Birds of the Atlantic Ocean

Birds of the Atlantic Ocean

Paintings by Keith Shackleton

Text by Ted Stokes

The Macmillan Company · New York

© 1968 by Ted Stokes & Keith Shackleton
All rights reserved. No part of this book may be reproduced or transmitted in any form or by any means, electronic or mechanical, including photocopying, recording or by any information storage and retrieval system, without permission in writing from the Publisher.

Library of Congress Catalog Card Number: 67-23527

First American Edition 1968

First published in Great Britain in 1968, for Country Life Books, by the Hamlyn Publishing Group Limited, Hamlyn House, Feltham, Middlesex

The Macmillan Company, New York

Printed in the Netherlands

AUTHOR'S DEDICATION

This book is dedicated in
all humility to all those who fight
to preserve and encourage
Nature's rarer members
and, in particular, to
Louis Mowbray and David Wingate
on whom the cahow depends
for its precarious existence

CONTENTS

List of identification plates 9

List of oil paintings 11

Author's Preface 13

Illustrator's Preface 14

ORDER *IMPENNES*

Family *Spheniscidae*—penguins 17

Emperor Penguin; Macaroni Penguin; Bearded Penguin; Adélie Penguin; King Penguin; Rockhopper Penguin; Gentoo Penguin; Jackass Penguin; Magellan Penguin

ORDER *TUBINARES*

Family *Diomedeidae*—albatrosses 24

Wandering Albatross; Royal Albatross; Black-browed Albatross; Shy Albatross; Grey-headed Albatross; Sooty Albatross; Light-mantled Sooty Albatross

Family *Procellariidae*—fulmars, prions, petrels, shearwaters 31

Giant Fulmar; Pintado; Antarctic Fulmar; Fulmar; Antarctic Petrel; Snow Petrel; Blue Petrel; Fairy Prion; Thin-billed Prion; Dove Prion; Broad-billed Prion; Great-winged Petrel; Schlegel's Petrel; Soft-plumaged Petrel; Kerguelen Petrel; Herald Petrel; Capped Petrel; Cahow; Bulwer's Petrel; Shoemaker; Cory's Shearwater; Pediunker; Tristan Great Shearwater; Sooty Shearwater; Manx Shearwater; Little Shearwater

Family *Hydrobatidae*—storm petrels 56

British Storm Petrel; Madeiran Storm Petrel; Leach's Storm Petrel; Wilson's Storm Petrel; White-faced Storm Petrel; Grey-backed Storm Petrel; Black-bellied Storm Petrel

Family *Pelecanoididae*—diving petrels 63

Common Diving Petrel; South Georgia Diving Petrel; Magellan Diving Petrel

ORDER *STEGANOPODES*

Family *Phaëthontidae*—tropic birds 66

Red-billed Tropic Bird; White-tailed Tropic Bird

Family *Pelecanidae*—pelicans 69

Pink-backed Pelican; American White Pelican; Brown Pelican

Family *Sulidae*—gannets and boobies 74

Northern Gannet; Cape Gannet; Blue-faced Booby; Red-footed Booby; Brown Booby

Family *Phalacrocoracidae*—cormorants 78

Double-crested Cormorant; Olivaceous Cormorant; Common Cormorant; Cape Cormorant; Bank Cormorant; Shag; Rock Shag; Red-footed Shag; Blue-eyed Shag; Reed Cormorant

Family *Fregatidae*—frigate birds 85

Ascension Frigate Bird; Magnificent Frigate Bird; Great Frigate Bird; Lesser Frigate Bird

ORDER *LARO-LIMICOLAE*

Family *Phalaropodidae*—phalaropes 90

Grey Phalarope; Wilson's Phalarope; Red-necked Phalarope

Family *Chionididae*—sheathbills 94

Sheathbill

Contents continued

Family *Stercorariidae*—skuas   95

Pomarine Skua; Arctic Skua; Long-tailed Skua; Great Skua

Family *Laridae*   100
Sub-family *Larinae*—gulls

Dominican Gull; Great Black-backed Gull; Glaucous Gull; Thayer's Gull; Iceland Gull; Herring Gull; Lesser Black-backed Gull; Common Gull; Ring-billed Gull; Audouin's Gull; Dolphin Gull; Great Black-headed Gull; Ivory Gull; Sabine's Gull; Ross's Gull; Little Gull; Black-headed Gull; Bonaparte's Gull; Slender-billed Gull; Grey-headed Gull; Silver Gull; Kittiwake; Laughing Gull; Franklin's Gull; Mediterranean Gull

Sub-family *Sterninae*—terns and noddies   124

Large-billed Tern; Little Tern; Black Tern; White-winged Black Tern; Whiskered Tern; Sooty Tern; Bridled Tern; Damara Tern; Trudeau's Tern; Forster's Tern; Arctic Tern; Antarctic Tern; South American Tern; Common Tern; Roseate Tern; Sandwich Tern; Lesser Crested Tern; Royal Tern; Caspian Tern; Gull-billed Tern; Common Noddy; White-capped Noddy; White Tern

Family *Rynchopidae*—skimmers   140

Black Skimmer, African Skimmer

Family *Alcidae*—auks   141

Dovekie; Razorbill; Guillemot; Arctic Guillemot; Black Guillemot; Puffin

Index   151

ILLUSTRATIONS

Identification Plates

Page 21 Penguins

Gentoo Penguin; King Penguin; Bearded Penguin; Macaroni Penguin; Magellan Penguin; Jackass Penguin; Emperor Penguin; Rockhopper Penguin; Adélie Penguin

Page 29 Albatrosses

Sooty Albatross; Grey-headed Albatross; Royal Albatross; Black-browed Albatross; Shy Albatross; Yellow-nosed Albatross; Wandering Albatross

Page 33 Petrels, Prions and Fulmars

Giant Fulmar; Fairy Prion; Thin-billed Prion; Pintado; Antarctic Petrel; Antarctic Fulmar; Blue Petrel

Page 41 Prions and Petrels

Dove Prion; Schlegel's Petrel; Great-winged Petrel; Herald Petrel; Kerguelen Petrel; Soft-plumaged Petrel; Broad-billed Prion

Page 49 Shearwaters and Petrels

Manx Shearwater; Cory's Shearwater; Pediunker; Little Shearwater; Sooty Shearwater; Shoemaker; Bulwer's Petrel; Capped Petrel

Page 61 Storm Petrels

Wilson's Storm Petrel; British Storm Petrel; Black-bellied Storm Petrel; Grey-backed Storm Petrel; Madeiran Storm Petrel; White-faced Storm Petrel

Page 67 Tropic Birds and Diving Petrels

Red-billed Tropic Bird; Common Diving Petrel; Magellan Diving Petrel

Page 71 Pelicans

American White Pelican; Brown Pelican; Pink-backed Pelican

Page 77 Gannets and Boobies

Cape Gannet; Brown Booby; Blue-faced Booby; Red-footed Booby

Page 83 Cormorants and Shags

Common Cormorant; Shag; Common Cormorant (southern type); Double-crested Cormorant; Olivacious Cormorant; Cape Cormorant; Bank Cormorant; Rock shag; Blue-eyed Shag; Reed Cormorant

Page 89 Frigate Birds

Magnificent Frigate Bird; Great Frigate Bird; Ascension Frigate Bird; Lesser Frigate Bird

Page 93 Phalaropes and Sheathbills

Red-necked Phalarope; Wilson's Phalarope; Grey Phalarope; Sheathbill

Page 97 Skuas

Pomarine Skua; Great Skua; Long-tailed Skua; Arctic Skua

Page 105 Gulls

Lesser Black-backed Gull; Iceland Gull; Common Gull; Great Black-backed Gull; Glaucous Gull; Audouin's Gull; Dominican Gull; Thayer's Gull; Ring-billed Gull

Page 109 Immature Gulls

Glaucous Gull; Iceland Gull; Lesser Black-backed Gull; Herring Gull; Great Black-backed Gull; Dominican Gull; Common Gull; Ring-billed Gull

Page 113 Immature Gulls

Ivory Gull; Little Gull; Dolphin Gull; Bonaparte's Gull; Sabine's Gull; Black-headed Gull; Ross's Gull

9

Page 115   Gulls

Ivory Gull; Little Gull; Dolphin Gull; Bonaparte's Gull; Sabine's Gull; Black-headed Gull; Ross's Gull

Page 117   Gulls

Mediterranean Gull; Franklin's Gull; Great Black-headed Gull

Page 121   Gulls

Silver Gull; Slender-billed Gull; Grey-headed Gull; Laughing Gull

Page 129   Terns
Damara Tern; Sooty Tern; Whiskered Tern; Large-billed Tern; Black Tern; Bridled Tern; White-winged Black Tern

Page 133   Terns

Forster's Tern; Trudeau's Tern; Common Tern; Arctic Tern; Antarctic Tern; South American Tern; Sandwich Tern

Page 135   Terns, Noddies and Skimmers

Caspian Tern; Royal Tern; Lesser Crested Tern; White Tern; Gull-billed Tern; Common Noddy; African Skimmer; White-capped Noddy

Page 143   Auks

Razorbill; Guillemot; Arctic Guillemot; Black Guillemot; Dovekie; Puffin

OIL PAINTINGS

	Page
Arctic Skuas	16
Wandering Albatross	25
Fulmar	35
Snow Petrel	37
Cahow	45
Tristan Great Shearwater	53
Leach's Storm Petrel	57
White-tailed Tropic Bird	65
Northern Gannet	73
Magnificent Frigate Bird	87
Herring Gull	101
Kittiwake	119
Little Tern	125
Roseate Tern	131
Black Skimmer	139

AUTHOR'S PREFACE

I was talking to the warden of an east coast bird sanctuary the other day, actually discussing the overlapping ranges of the common and arctic terns, and he made a remark which stuck firmly in my mind.

'You see, sir,' he said, 'I am not an ornithologist, I'm a naturalist, I know my birds intimately – have done all my life – but scientific classification and the like mean precious little to me.'

I know exactly what he meant. Since before I can remember, birds and their recognition have been second nature to me, but I could never claim to be an ornithologist – not a scientific one.

A complete study of ocean birds, however, is impossible without considerable reliance on science. I have had as much opportunity for ocean travel as most, but I have never seen many of the birds featured in this book. The subject has been covered, either in whole or in part, by many greater and more knowledgeable writers than myself. From their works I have gleaned a lot of the information, though much of it is personal observation. It is in the realm of illustration that past publications on the subject have, perhaps, fallen short of this book. Keith Shackleton's paintings must, surely, be the most complete collection of illustrations of ocean birds ever published. I am mighty proud, therefore, to have been asked to write the text for what is, without question, a major contribution to ornithological illustration.

In deference to the scientists, the birds in this book are arranged in their correct scientific order. Each species is accompanied by a map showing, in black, its known breeding range and, in grey, the probable limits of its non-breeding range.

The maps are, perforce, small, so the reader cannot expect to pinpoint any particular breeding site from them. They do, however, give a fair idea of whether you can expect to see any particular bird in any particular area, or not.

The only dimensions I have given – except in the case of penguins – are mean wing spans. Birds, after all, are usually seen on the wing at sea and this dimension gives a rough guide. A word of warning though; sizes are very deceptive over the ocean and the beginner could be forgiven for grossly under-estimating span. An albatross, for instance, doesn't look all that big when it follows effortlessly in the wake of a ship. Yet the biggest ones have a span of anything up to twelve feet! There are cases, of course, where the span of the male and female of a species differ. I have given only one figure which is the mean, but in such cases – frigate birds, for instance – I have mentioned sex size variation in the text.

With each bird, I have given some of the commoner synonyms by which they are known. I shall be told, I know, that I have used the wrong primary English name for some birds. This, surely, is a matter of choice and I have used the names which I have been brought up with and have not deferred to organised ornithological practice. It is not ignorance, just pig-headedness!

Finally, a word of appreciation. I have culled my information from many sources, both expert and in-expert but local. Five people, however, I would like to thank very specially for their help. They are R. M. Lockley, James Fisher, Louis Mowbray, David Wingate and Ralph Palmer. Their kindness to a mere amateur has been boundless.

Droxford, 1967

T.S.

ILLUSTRATOR'S PREFACE

The ocean birds have no gaudy plumage. In painting the whole series of their portraits the mixed up colours in daily use have varied through white, brown and grey to black. Brighter accents have been noticeable for their stark economy and enriched by the drabness of their setting. The occasional sealing-wax red of a tern's bill or the gular sack of a frigate bird, the vivid green of a shag's eye, have been details to break the monotony of what would otherwise have been a dreary palette.

It is in their drawing that these birds have most to offer. Their trim, functional lines are of the kind one sees borrowed by designers of the best boats and aeroplanes, yet despite being moulded for a maritime need their shapes are as varied as most birds of the land. A fickle task-master, the ocean has guided a trend of evolution for those who live off her bounty, with scope enough to make the flightless penguin equally as successful an animal as the long-winged albatross. There are cormorants and pelicans, endearing for their very ugliness, and there are tropic birds, which if I had to make so hard a choice, I would name the most beautiful birds that fly.

A method of presentation has been a problem. These particular groups show little difference in the sexes, though many have great changes in plumage between young and old. Again such a degree of individual variation exists, even among adults of certain species, that a single illustration may never hope to be entirely correct – though it may equally claim never to be entirely wrong.

There are albatrosses with upper parts predominately white with black wing-tips and trailing edges. Their young are brownish grey. Yet one may travel for days at sea and watch a hundred birds, each one demonstrating its own variation on a theme of pied or chequer-board design, and be left with the feeling that no two albatrosses are alike. Some of the skuas and petrels have a distinct light and dark phase, with typical examples of each form easy to tell apart. Yet there seem always to be the indeterminate variants that would be hard to place in either group. Moreover, variation is not confined to colour alone, but in a lesser degree to size and outline, the detailed profile of the bill; and just as with land birds, there are separate species whose superficial appearance, even in the hand, is all but the same.

Many of these birds I have been lucky enough to see alive. The others are in groups the characteristics of which are fairly familiar either from detailed description and comparison or from representatives of their genus nearer home. I have tried to draw them as faithfully as I can, sorting through very large numbers of skins in an effort to pick an average adult bird to represent each subject. Often I have wished there was space enough to draw several and illustrate a fuller range of their markings, but now the work is complete I can only testify to the importance of the written word, for in many cases my contribution has gone no further than a general note of character and appearance for each subject.

There are fifteen oil paintings, all of single species against their backgrounds of sea and sky. The remaining twenty-three plates are drawings in gouache composed as a series of group portraits, enlarging where possible upon points of special interest or details that set one bird noticeably apart from another. In some cases this has led to drawing the head alone, as with the terns, for this is where the significant differences lie. In others I have enlarged a head or bill out of scale with the rest of the page, to offer a clearer view of structure. In the case of the giant fulmar, the bird is so much larger than its relatives that they would have had little showing if the whole spread of wings had been drawn. Compromise has been inevitable for I can think of no other way to set out so many varied studies in a simple uniform plan.

References for this work have come from individual travellers and naturalists, from expeditions and weather ships, lighthouses and polar bases. Often the label which a specimen bore was as evocative as the bird itself. I found myself drawing from a petrel skin prepared by Dr Wilson on Captain Scott's last Antarctic expedition in the *Terranova*. To have access to such research has been essential and for this I am deeply grateful to the Trustees and Bird Room staff of the British Museum of Natural History for their generous help, interest – and patience!

For me the rewards have been many. There is a timely discipline for a painter in preparing illustrations instead of pictures. There is new stimulus in trying to be creative within a circumscribed mandate. But most rewarding of all has been the necessity for a more clinical approach to a subject I have always held dear and which I shall never tire of painting. The ocean birds have all the romance a subject can offer. They bewitch us and humiliate us with their unassuming mastery of wind, water and whereabouts. They provide inspiration and example for mariners and aeronauts alike, but that is not all. Since man first ventured into their domain they have offered the solace of live company and visual delight where their need is greatest.

London, W.11, 1967.   K.S.

ORDER *IMPENNES*

FAMILY *SPHENISCIDAE* – PENGUINS

Penguins are so well known to most people that a general description of their appearance seems almost superfluous. The smart, flightless birds of children's books, the comic strip, the toyshop and some zoos, standing upright with white waiters' shirt-fronts and arm-like flippers, are familiar to us all. Yet relatively few people have seen a penguin in its natural habitat and fewer still have made a close study of their lives.

The name, penguin, is what sailors used to call the great auk; now unhappily extinct. When a vaguely similar flightless bird, with upright stance and wings which could serve only as aids to swimming, was encountered in the Antarctic seas, the sailors naturally gave it the same name. There is no relationship between the two families, but the name has stuck.

EMPEROR PENGUIN

Aptenodytes forsteri

Length 43 inches.

The emperor is the largest member of the penguin family. It is also the most truly Antarctic species, breeding as it does on the fast ice of the Antarctic continent. A tall, upright bird, it has a blue-grey back and white front. The head and cheeks are jet black and the sides of the neck are a brilliant yellow. Its bill is long, sharp and down-curved, with the black feathers of the face extending well along the lower mandible. A distinct black border band runs down from each shoulder to the leading edge of the flippers.

Not only does the emperor breed on the Antarctic ice, but it lays its one pale bluish-white egg at the height of the Antarctic winter, in late June or early July. The bird incubates its egg holding it between the tops of its feet and the underside of its loose-skinned belly. Colonies of brooding birds stand huddled together in large numbers, withstanding the worst that the bitter southern winter can offer.

Young emperors hatch in September. By January, they have lost most of their silver-grey down and are almost as tall as their parents. In the meantime, however, they have already started their annual northerly migration. Having wandered down onto the edge of the sea ice with their parents in November, they are forcibly put to sea by the spring break-up of the ice. Like commuting passengers on a harbour ferry, they stand patiently together while the rafts of ice carry them north.

The emperors' northerly migration in the Antarctic summer does not take them north of the latitude of the South Orkneys. It is a time for constant and gluttonous fish eating, however, for they must stoke

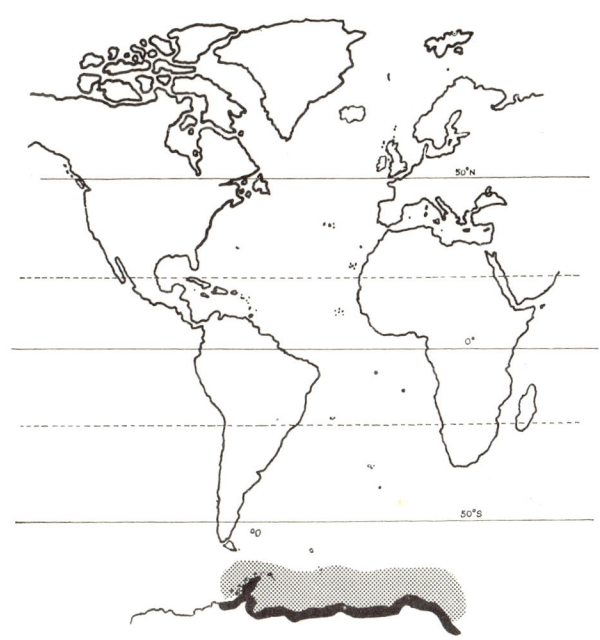

Arctic Skuas

BIRDS OF THE ATLANTIC OCEAN

up for the long periods of fast in the next breeding season.

Emperor penguins normally walk upright on land. If disturbed or harried, however, they fling themselves flat on their faces and propel themselves with flying feet and flippers at speeds of up to twenty miles an hour; a comic and colourful exposition of the French expression *ventre à terre*.

Macaroni penguins may be encountered anywhere in the Southern Atlantic Ocean out of the breeding season where they will be swimming far from land, sometimes diving for fish, sometimes resting low in the water with little more than their heads showing.

This is a bird of the southern oceans, but not of the true Antarctic; not a bird of the frozen continent.

MACARONI PENGUIN

Eudyptes chrysolophus

Length 27 inches

This is a medium-sized penguin with dark grey back, black head, chin and throat. There are long plumes, orange with black tips, across the forehead and above and behind each eye. The underparts are white and the bill is black with a red tip; pink and naked at the base.

Macaroni penguins breed on most of the islands of the Antarctic Ocean; South Shetland, South Orkney, South Georgia, the Falklands, South Sandwich, Bouvet and Crozet Islands. Three eggs of the usual pale penguin blue-green – almost spherical in shape – are laid in November on the tussock-covered slopes of these lonely islands. They hatch towards the end of December and the chicks take to the water six to ten weeks after hatching.

In places where their range overlaps, the members of this species and rockhopper penguins nest together in large mixed colonies.

BEARDED PENGUIN
(Syns: ringed penguin. chinstrap penguin)
Pygoscelis antarcticia

Length 30 inches.

James Weddell, the explorer, called this penguin the stone cracker because of its ear splitting ejaculation, *'ah crrack'*. The Spaniards call it *pinguin de barbijo; barbijo* being the strap which passes under the chin and holds the gaucho's hat. The English and American names are self-explanatory as the bird, which is mainly grey on top and white underneath, has this marked black line which extends from the nape of the neck under the chin like a W. W. Jacobs fisherman's beard.

The bearded penguin is the most pugnacious of all penguins. Some ignore man when he intrudes upon their privacy, some run coyly away, but this fellow attacks fiercely whenever opportunity occurs.

Two greenish-white eggs are laid in late November and the young hatch in January. They already have the chinstraps by February. The nest is a simple ring

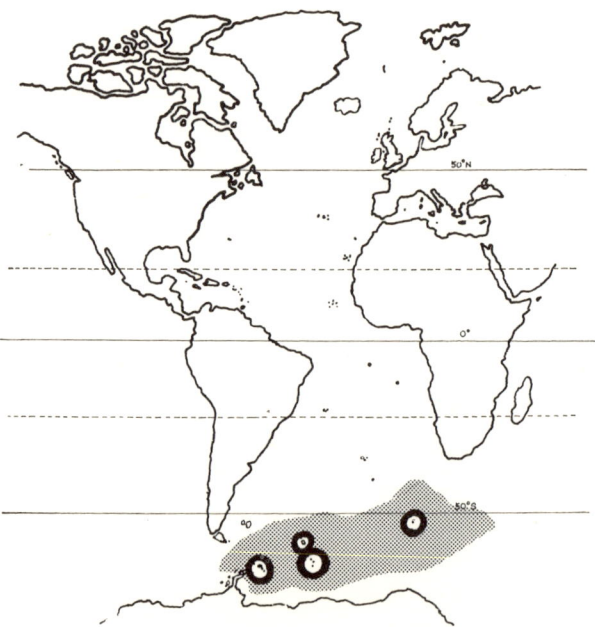

18

of just sufficient stones to stop the eggs rolling away from the slight depression in which they are laid.

There are colonies of this species on Bouvet, South Orkney and South Sandwich Islands and South Georgia. Out of the breeding season they range throughout the South Atlantic and adjacent Antarctic seas.

ADÉLIE PENGUIN

Pygoscelis adeliae

Length 28 inches.

The Adélie penguin is blue-black on top and white beneath. The head, cheeks and throat are jet black, but the eyelids are white, giving a nigger minstrel effect. It is a bird of far more southerly range than the previous two species, nesting on the coast of Antarctica and nearby islands and only wandering north as far as South Georgia. The name is derived from Madame Adélie Durville, after whom the bird was originally named.

Adélies nest in fairly large colonies, laying two eggs in October. The nests are made by piling stones up together into a miniature volcano-like mound. Much scrapping goes on at nesting time over the ownership of stones; sometimes to the detriment of eggs which are quickly snapped up by the ever attendant skuas. The young hatch in December and are ready to go to sea in February.

Being a bird of the far south, the Adélie has to survive many a blizzard while incubating its eggs. They have been known, at this time, to become completely snowed over without serious harm. Mortality, however, is very high, for not only do the gulls and skuas prey on the eggs and young, but the Adélie is a favourite meal of the fearsome leopard seal which lurks in wait off the shoreline at the time the birds take to the sea again when breeding is over.

The Adélie is capable of the most fantastic leaps from the water. One of the finest spectacles of the Antarctic is provided when they come ashore for breeding, bird after bird shooting out of the water like a Polaris missile and landing firmly on its feet, high on the plateau of ice which is the shoreline.

When an Adélie's eggs are stolen, she lays again like a sensible barnyard hen. This, presumably, is one of the reasons why the species, in spite of constant casualties from predation, survives in such large numbers. When at sea the Adélie penguin swims with its back submerged so that only its head shows above water.

KING PENGUIN

Aptenodytes patagonica

Length 38 inches.

The king is like the emperor penguin only smaller. The colouring on the neck and cheeks is more orange on the adult bird and the base of the lower mandible is red and not feathered. The bill is longer and also more slender, in comparison to the size of the bird.

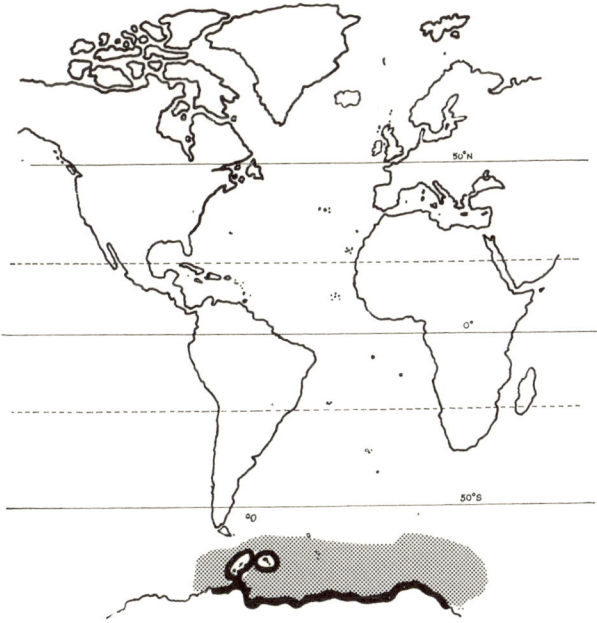 

BIRDS OF THE ATLANTIC OCEAN

King penguins, who do not have such a southern range as the emperors, march very upright with their bills held high like a platoon of well-drilled soldiers. Like emperors, they make no nest, but hold their one pure white egg between their feet and the fold of skin at the base of the belly. The egg, though white when laid, soon becomes very muddy and discoloured as breeding takes place not on ice in the Antarctic winter, but on bare soil in the Antarctic summer. Eggs are laid in November or December and vary enormously in size from bird to bird.

Breeding colonies exist on Staten Island, off the tip of Tierra del Fuego, on South Georgia, and on the Falklands and Sandwich Islands. Unlike most penguins they are not migratory. The sea never freezes around their nesting colonies and they have no need to wander far to catch their main diet of squid.

ROCKHOPPER PENGUIN

Eudyptes crestatus

Length 24 inches.

So called because it bounds about on land as if progressing on a pogo stick, this penguin breeds on Tristan da Cunha, Gough Island and the coast of Tierra del Fuego. It is the penguin with the largest crest of all. Long, pale yellow plumes running from behind the nostrils, over the eyes and blowing out behind, give the bird a children's party look.

They have short, thick, orange or red bills and

1. Gentoo Penguin. 2. King Penguin. 3. Bearded Penguin.
4. Macaroni Penguin. 5. Magellan Penguin. 6. Jackass Penguin.
7. Emperor Penguin. 8. Rockhopper Penguin.
9. Adélie Penguin.

pale feet with very dark webs.

Their nests are built in large, congested colonies; just simple scoops in the ground, lined with grass and twigs. Two pale green eggs are laid in October or November and the young hatch in December, departing to sea in March or April. Rockhopper and macaroni penguins are sometimes found in mixed colonies.

GENTOO PENGUIN

Pygoscelis papua

Length 30 inches.

Affectionately known as 'Johnny' penguin, the gentoo is the only penguin with white on top of its head. A white patch extends upwards from each eye meeting over the crown. In the Atlantic sector of the

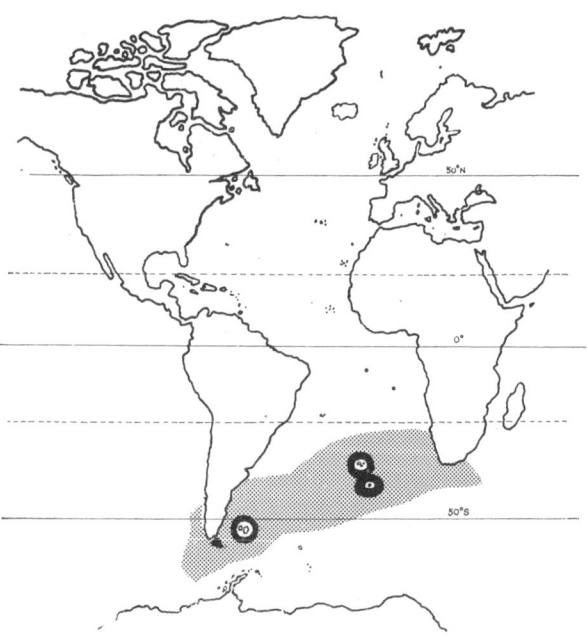

BIRDS OF THE ATLANTIC OCEAN

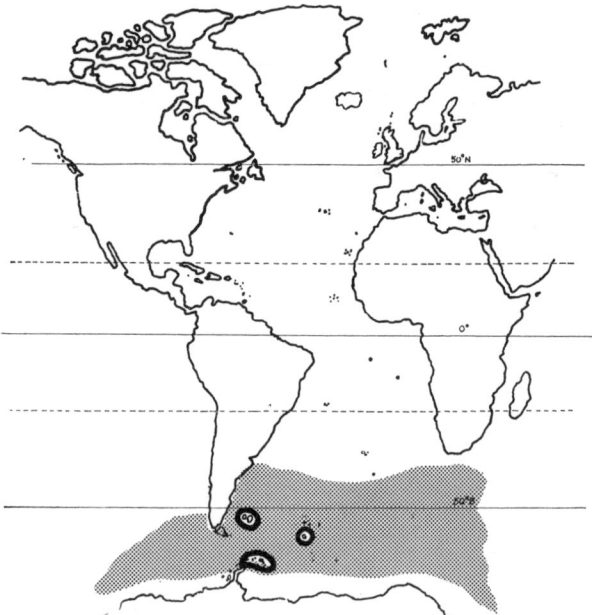
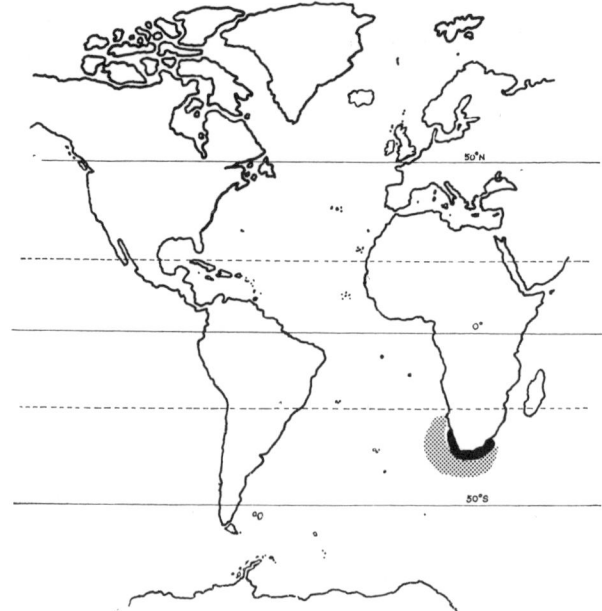

southern oceans, the bird breeds on South Georgia and the Falkland Islands. It seems to have a built-in urge to climb. To some extent, a lot of the smaller penguins have this, but the gentoo climbs to greater heights – sometimes over 1,000 feet above sea level – to nest.

Every year, in late September, the birds come ashore and make the long trek up the mountain-side over well worn tracks and melting snowfields. The nests are mounds of humus among high tussocks of coarse grass. Two greenish-white eggs are laid in October and the average incubation period is thirty-three days.

The gentoo is the commonest and most timid of all penguins. When seen at sea, it floats low in the water with not much more than its head showing, but is always recognisable by the diagnostic brilliant white headband.

JACKASS PENGUIN

Spheniscus demersus

Length 25 inches.

This, the south African penguin, is called jackass because of the harsh bray-like call uttered when the birds are congregated at the rookery. The bird has a thick, almost razorbill-like beak. A white stripe runs back from the bill, above the eye, curving round to join the white of the chest, leaving an 'island' patch of black on the throat. There is a narrow horseshoe band over the chest, running down each side to the feet. The band, the back and flippers, the beak and the throat patch are quite black, so that the bird is strikingly black and white.

Jackass penguins breed on islands off the south African coast, laying their three pale greeny-white eggs in May and June for the most part, but there are some birds breeding at almost all seasons of the year.

When at sea, this species spends a lot of time lying on the surface of the water, its body horizontal, its flippers outstretched and the bill pointed skywards at an angle of about 45°. Like all penguins, it is a frequent sleeper! When diving it goes straight down without leaving the water.

MAGELLAN PENGUIN

Spheniscus magellanicus

Length 27 inches.

The Magellan penguin is similar in facial marking to the jackass penguin. The throat patch is black, but the back and flipper-tops are browny-grey. The horseshoe band on the breast is considerably broader. The two species cannot, of course, be confused as they inhabit completely different parts of the world.

Not only is the general pattern of colouring similar between these two species, but the Magellan penguin

ORDER *IMPENNES*

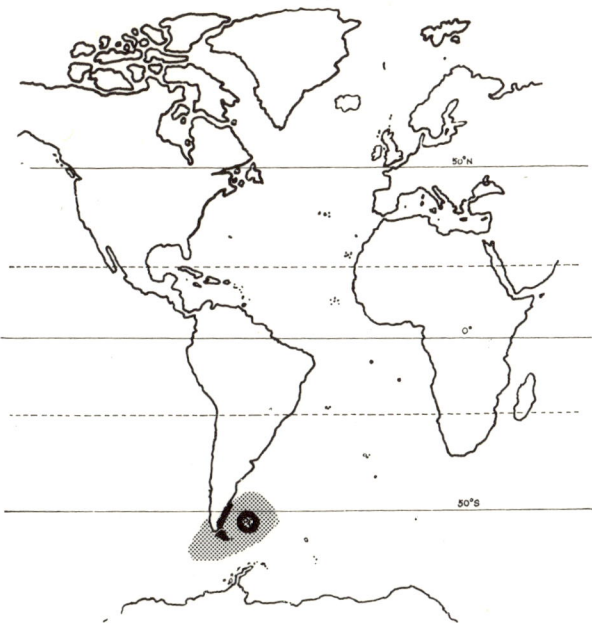

is known in South America as the 'jackass' because of its bray-like call.

Nesting in burrows on the Falkland Islands and on the Patagonian coast right down to Cape Horn, *magellanicus* lays two eggs, starting in October. The young hatch in November or early December and are away to sea by March.

For a penguin, the bird floats high and horizontal when surfaced, beak raised skywards, dozing frequently like a fat holiday-maker on a lilo mattress. Under water, however, the story is very different. Like all penguins they swim at great speeds and with incredible manoeuvrability.

ORDER *TUBINARES*

FAMILY *DIOMEDEIDAE* – ALBATROSSES

Every young sailor with a soul, with the tiniest spark of romance in his being, wants one day to see an albatross. The albatross, the bird of myth and mystery, the bird of the legend of the Ancient Mariner, is surely the symbol of ultimate achievement and maturity in the mind of all but the dullest of seafaring folk. For, in these days of aeroplane and steamship, of short cuts and canals, few of the world's travellers touch albatross country; that is left to real sailors.

Albatrosses inhabit the great oceans of the south where uninterrupted water girdles the earth and strong westerly winds blow unceasingly. Their only venturings north to waters frequented by man are mainly in those longtitudes where the east-going ocean drifts branch north along the west coasts of the main continental masses, though, in the Pacific, some species do migrate regularly north of the equator and one species actually breeds on the equator, in the Galapagos Islands.

The largest sea birds – in fact, the largest surviving flying creatures – albatrosses have heavy bodies and relatively narrow wings. Their heads are large, their necks longish, their tails short. Their bills are remarkable, being stout and hooked and made up of a number of plates. The nostrils are in the form of flat louvres each side of the upper mandible. Albatrosses belong to the order *TUBINARES,* tubenoses, but the tubes are not as obvious as those of petrels and shearwaters.

WANDERING ALBATROSS

Diomedea exulans

Wing span 122 inches.

This is the real albatross, the albatross of the Ancient Mariner. It is an enormous bird with a wing span of anything up to twelve feet. The old male birds are pure white with a broad black border to the wings. The adult female has a small dark patch on the crown. But don't be dismayed if you see a wandering albatross which is far from white. It takes the average wanderer at least ten years – probably longer – to attain full, snow-white maturity of plumage, and the stages passed through to reach maturity are very variable. The youngest birds are nearly entirely brown on top, though white under the wings. Then, by gradual degrees, more white and less brown shows on the back until the perfect and, unfortunately, all too infrequently seen state of full plumage is reached.

Wanderers breed on Tristan da Cunha, Gough Island and South Georgia. They lay one large, chalky-white, pear-shaped egg speckled with red, on a mound of grass and mud. Breeding birds come in from the ocean in November or December and the eggs are usually laid by Christmas. The young hatch in March and are fed continuously by one parent or the other until about June. By then they are large and fat and clad in a thick woolly down. The parents then go off to sea and the young bird is left sitting on its nest where it remains, by itself, right through the Antarctic winter.

The opinions of authorities vary about this stage in the young albatross's life. Murphy says that they are not fed between June and December, when the old birds return. Richdale believes the old birds

BIRDS OF THE ATLANTIC OCEAN

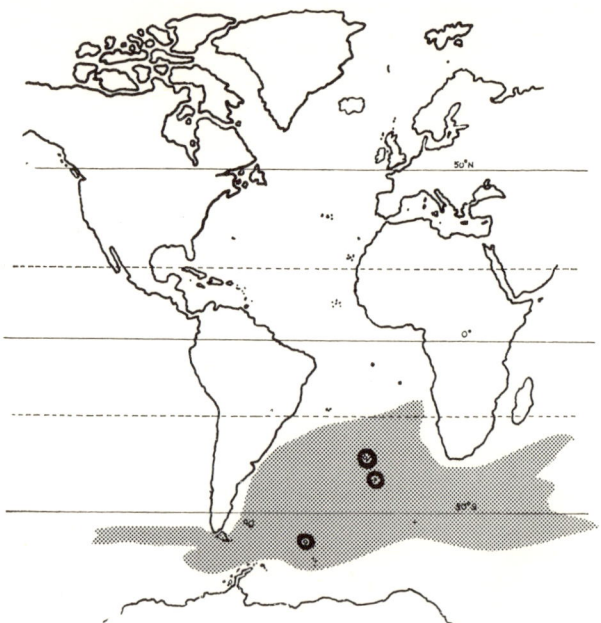
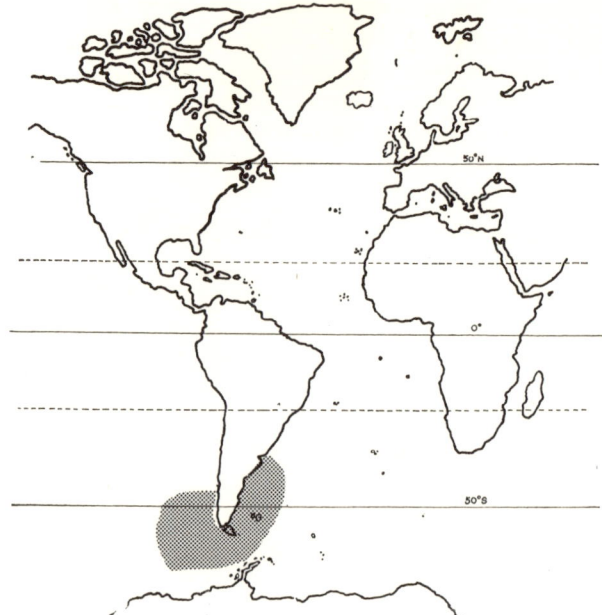

continue to feed their young, albeit at very infrequent intervals. No one seems to know for certain, as the Antarctic winter, though it may not defeat the young albatross sitting on the nest in a state of semi-hibernation, has so far effectively prevented accurate and prolonged observation by man.

The old birds returning in the spring will take no notice of the young, who eventually push off to sea, leaving their parents engrossed in the business of raising a fresh family.

Birds probably mate for life, but out of the breeding season they wander thousands of miles over the face of the southern oceans; usually singly.

ROYAL ALBATROSS

Diomedea epomophora

Wing span 118 inches.

Very little is known about this member of the albatross family. To look at, it is similar to the male wandering albatross in full, adult plumage; entirely white except for the black primaries. There may be a few grey mottles, but nothing to notice at any distance. The bill and the feet are paler than those of *exulans* and also the bill is slightly more slender. It is thus practically impossible to differentiate the two species when they are sighted at sea.

Safe to say, however, that a monstrous white albatross with considerable, irregular patches of dark on its back is a wandering albatross; an all-white bird with black primaries is either a wandering albatross or a royal albatross. Where the bird is seen may be some clue. In the eastern half of the south Atlantic you are unlikely to encounter a royal albatross, for they nest high in the inaccessible interior of Tierra del Fuego and in the antipodes, and therefore qualify as Atlantic birds only at the far eastern limit of their range.

D. epomophora and *D. exulans* overlap at sea only in the vicinity of Cape Horn and up the eastern seaboard of South America as far as Uruguay.

The single, large, white egg with a darker zone at one end is laid any time from November to January. The whole process of bringing up young from egg to independence takes over a year, so in each alternate year there is a short non-breeding season.

BLACK-BROWED ALBATROSS

Diomedea melanophris

Wing span 90 inches.

The black-browed albatross is a beautiful bird of regular, clear-cut marking. The disappointing thing about the wandering albatross, to an enthusiast seeing one for the first time, is the untidy, blotchy effect of the varying back plumage. Not so with the black-browed albatross. He is a smart fellow with pure white head and undersides, and clearly defined dark back. Almost as though conscious of his good looks he is ever so slightly 'made up', having a dark grey line running over and accentuating the eye. From this feature, of course, he gets his name. The bird also has a rich yellow bill to complete the picture.

D. melanophris breeds on South Georgia and the Falkland Islands. As with all of the albatross family, the egg is large and whitish. It is laid any time between September and Christmas.

All albatrosses are, to a certain extent, wandering birds and some cover enormous mileages. The frequent reports of black-browed albatrosses in the North Atlantic – nine within the last seventy years – suggest that this species wanders well north when not engaged on family matters. After all, the North Atlantic is an enormous tract of ocean. If a battleship can disappear for days on end in it, as has happened more than once in recent naval history, how many of a particular species of bird must there be in this vast empty space for there to be regular sighting reports?

Not many, perhaps, but it seems possible that this bird is a regular visitor north of the equator. The only argument which might be set against this is that the black-browed albatross is an inveterate follower of ships, so that if it did regularly travel as far north as the trade routes of the North Atlantic, then sightings would be far more frequent. Who knows? There is such a lot of ocean in the world and so little that man knows about it.

The fact remains that black-browed albatrosses are seen or picked up or shot on far northern Atlantic shores, and sometimes inland, with what appears to be some pattern of regularity. Most of these appearances are due, no doubt, to accident. When a bird appears by accident a 100 or 200 miles from its habitat, there is nothing remarkable. If, however, it keeps popping up 5,000 miles from where it is meant to be, surely it is not an accident to the bird but a gap in man's knowledge.

SHY ALBATROSS
Diomedea cauta

Wing span 96 inches.

Most albatrosses tend to follow ships for long spells. There are stories of birds doing this for days on end, gliding back and forth across the wake. It certainly appears so, for there they are, as darkness falls, beautiful great creatures, wheeling and banking on long straight wings, close to, but never quite touching the waves. Then, there they are the following morning, still in attendance.

If they are the same birds at dusk and dawn, they must fly day and night without sleep for, possibly, a week on end. It is a theory which has never been proved or disproved, but experts are of the opinion that, when a ship is in albatross latitudes, birds will follow out of curiosity and certainly also to pick up refuse from the ship for a day and then go off at dark, settling on the water for sleep. They say that the next morning, a new lot of birds see the ship and join up to follow. This opinion is based on the fact that, at first light, there may be only one or two in sight, and then throughout the day they may

increase so that by later afternoon, their numbers might reach twenty.

Be that as it may, the shy albatross is so called because it does not follow ships.

The bird is completely white beneath. The head, neck and back are greyish-brown, the bill dull yellow with black at the base of the upper mandible and orange at the base of the lower mandible. The feet are a chilly flesh-colour. There is a line over the eye, but this is not quite as marked as on the black-browed albatross.

Cauta is not an Atlantic breeder, but is sometimes seen in fairly large concentrations off the west coast of south Africa, where it apparently congregates in June or July. It breeds in the south Pacific, egg dates being from August to October.

GREY-HEADED ALBATROSS

(Syn.: yellow-nosed albatross)

Diomedea chrysostoma

(D. chlororhynchos)

Wing span 80 inches.

Grey-headed albatross is the specific name of the bird, although the race, *D. chlororhynchos*, the yellow-nosed albatross, is the one concerned in Atlantic distribution. The bird is a dark, sooty, brownish-grey on its back. The undersides are white except that there is a broad dark border to the undersides of the wings. The head is white except for a marked

1. Sooty Albatross. 2. Grey-headed Albatross.
3. Royal Albatross. 4. Black-browed Albatross.
5. Manx Shearwater. 6. Shy Albatross.
7. Yellow-nosed Albatross. 8. Wandering Albatross.

grey patch. The bill is black with a yellow line down it; orange at the tip. The feet are bluish flesh-colour.

Yellow-nosed albatrosses breed on Tristan da Cunha and Gough Island and lay the usual one chalky-white egg in late September or early October.

It has the northernmost range, outside the breeding season, of any Atlantic albatross and so is the most likely to be encountered on any of the normal South Atlantic shipping routes.

SOOTY ALBATROSS

(Syn.: dark-mantled sooty albatross)

Diomedea fusca

Wing span 78 inches.

This is another albatross which breeds in the Tristan da Cunha group and at Gough Island. It is, however, an all dark bird as the name implies, being dark,

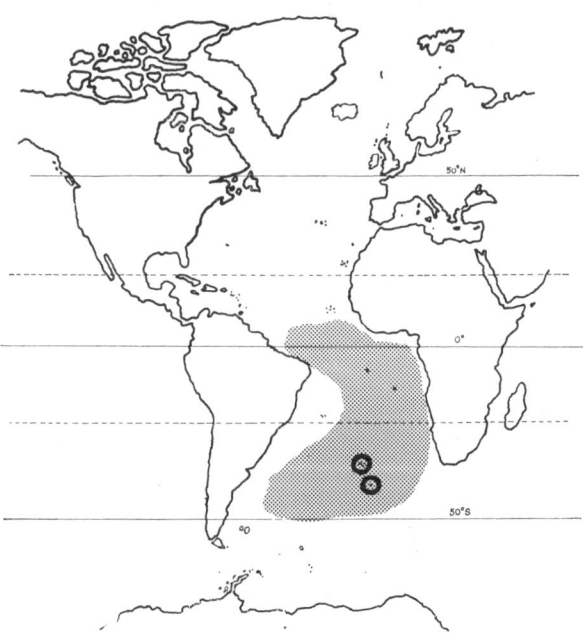

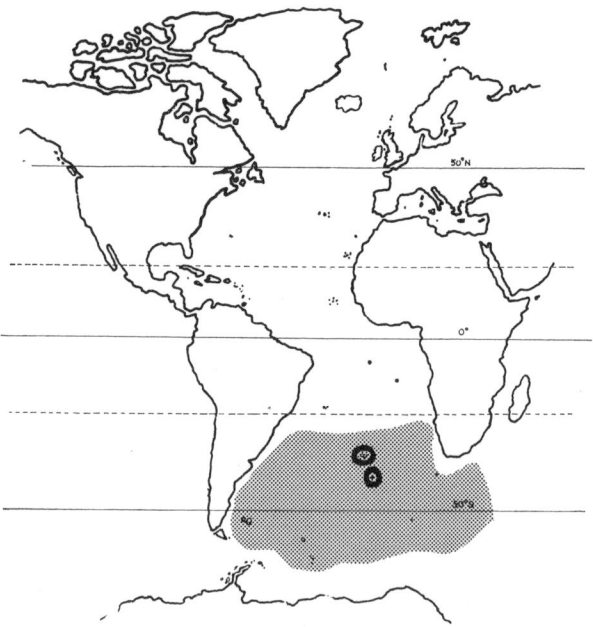
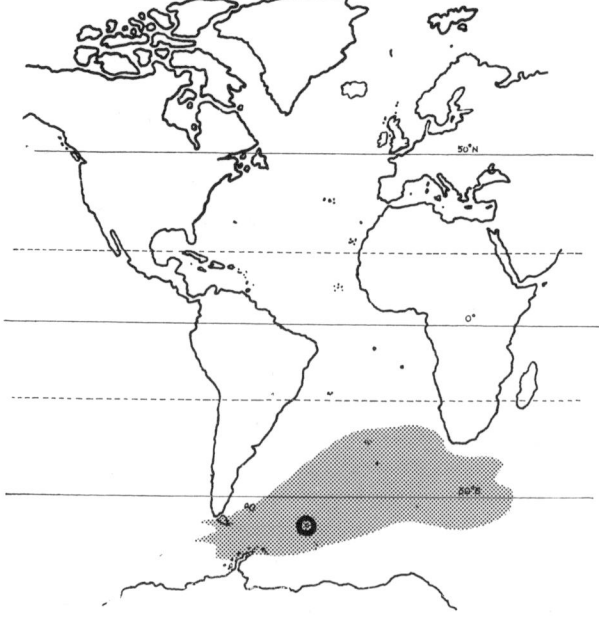

sooty-brown on the wings and face and only slightly paler beneath and in the centre of the back. There is a white horseshoe around the eye and the tail is long and wedge-shaped. Incidentally it is this wedge-shaped tail which makes differentiation certain between this species and the young of the wandering albatross. It is difficult – almost impossible – to judge the size of a single bird over the ocean and sometimes very difficult to note more than the main pattern of coloration in the changing lights of a moderate sea. So watch for the wedge tail, to be certain.

Out of the breeding season, which is from September to January, the birds range anywhere from the ice edge, north to latitude 30°S., not far south of the tropic of Capricorn, so well within the region of normal shipping routes to South America and south Africa.

LIGHT-MANTLED SOOTY ALBATROSS

Diomedea palpebrata

Wing span 78 inches.

There is considerable confusion of opinion among scientists whether the light-mantled sooty albatross is a separate species from the sooty albatross or not. They are, it is true, different in coloration, but they do not overlap in their breeding grounds, the sooty being more a bird of the Pacific. South Georgia is the only Atlantic island on which they breed. It seems possible, therefore, that they are well-marked geographical races of the same species.

Very like *D. fusca,* the light-mantled sooty albatross varies in that, as its name suggests, the mantle – the portion of its back between its wings – is much paler. The head is darker, too, making the effect of the light mantle even more marked by contrast. Both *D. fusca* and *D. palpebrata* have black bills with a contrasting groove along the side of the lower mandible, but *palpebrata*'s is pale blue while *fusca*'s is yellow. The white eye horseshoe is common to both birds.

This bird lays its eggs in October, which is a month later than the previous species, but South Georgia is twelve hundred miles further south than both Tristan and Gough, so the different season is still no argument for separating them specifically.

The latest edict of the scientists, however, is two species; so two species they are in this book!

ORDER *TUBINARES*

FAMILY *PROCELLARIIDAE*

This family is one of the largest of all ocean bird groups. It includes fulmars, prions, petrels and shearwaters. The only tubenoses outside the family are albatrosses and storm petrels. The only family which numerically exceeds this one is *Laridae,* gulls and terns, and they are by no means entirely marine and not, in any true sense, pelagic.

All the members of the family spend a large part of their life at sea and come to land only in the breeding season. They feed on fish and plankton and, in some cases, refuse from ships. Some migrate enormous distances; some stay within a few hundred miles of their nesting sites.

They are all slow breeders. With very few exceptions they lay one large egg; large, that is, in comparison with the size of the bird. Incubation and fledging periods are very protracted.

All are strong fliers, having rather long, straight wings, and most fly with great skill very close to the surface of the ocean, taking full advantage of the varying air currents associated with the waves. So close do some fly to the surface that they sometimes appear to wipe their wing tips on the water. All swim well and most of them dive.

Nearly all breed in burrows, though some are forced by circumstances or by local conditions to breed in rock crevices or on cliff ledges. Only the largest breed in the unprotected open. They apparently mate for life, although it is now thought that this comes about only because each individual returns to the same nest, thus meeting the same partner when the urge to reproduce is strongest. It is doubtful if any stay together as pairs out of the breeding season.

Sub-family *Fulmarinae* – fulmars and allies

GIANT FULMAR
Macronectes giganteus

Wing span 84 inches.

Traditionally known to sailors as 'Nelly' or 'Stinker', this enormous bird is distinguishable from the albatrosses by its heavier, clumsier appearance. The tubes on the nose, too, are quite separate and distinct, like two forward pointing guns, not faired in like an albatross's.

There are two colour phases, one nearly white and one dark. The light phase birds, which have a more southerly range, are more or less spotted with pale brown, while the dark phase birds are chocolate brown with paler head and breast. The large bill is straw-coloured and the feet brown or black.

Unlike most of the petrel family, the giant fulmar breeds on open tracts of ground – sometimes sandy, sometimes grassy. Some of their colonies are vast and, in spite of the enormous size of the bird, are still perilously susceptible to the attentions of

BIRDS OF THE ATLANTIC OCEAN

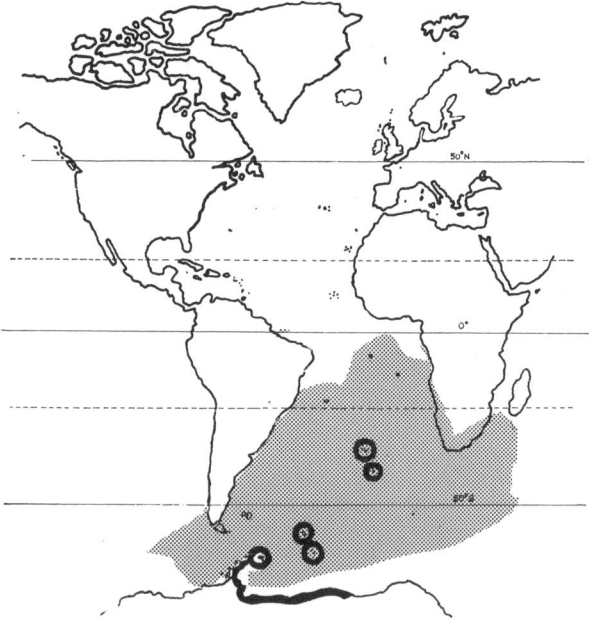

predatory gulls and skuas, who are quick to snap up unattended eggs.

A single, large, white, pointed egg is laid any time from September to January. Fledging time, as with all *TUBINARES,* is long and protracted.

From their breeding grounds on the Antarctic continent, South Shetland, South Orkney, Tristan da Cunha, Gough Island, the Falklands and South Georgia, they disperse over the southern oceans as far north as Capricorn. They can frequently be seen in large flocks in the busier harbours of the southern hemisphere as, like their small cousin the fulmar of northern latitudes, they are incorrigible scavengers.

1. Giant Fulmar (white phase). 2. Fairy Prion.
3. Thin-billed Prion. 4. Pintado. 5. Antarctic Petrel.
6. Antarctic Fulmar. 7. Blue Petrel.
8. Giant Fulmar (brown phase).

PINTADO

(Syn.: Cape pigeon)

Fulmarus (Daption) capensis

Wing span 34 inches.

Sooner or later, the ocean voyager travelling south from the latitude of Gibraltar towards the tropics and on, into the southern oceans, will be bound to see a dumpy, strikingly piebald, pigeon-like bird ranging effortlessly and apparently aimlessly, low over the waves. Though pintados do not generally appear to follow ships, they are probably by far the most frequently seen southern ocean bird. This may be because they like to fly in the vicinity of ships or just because they are so numerous. Their contrasting

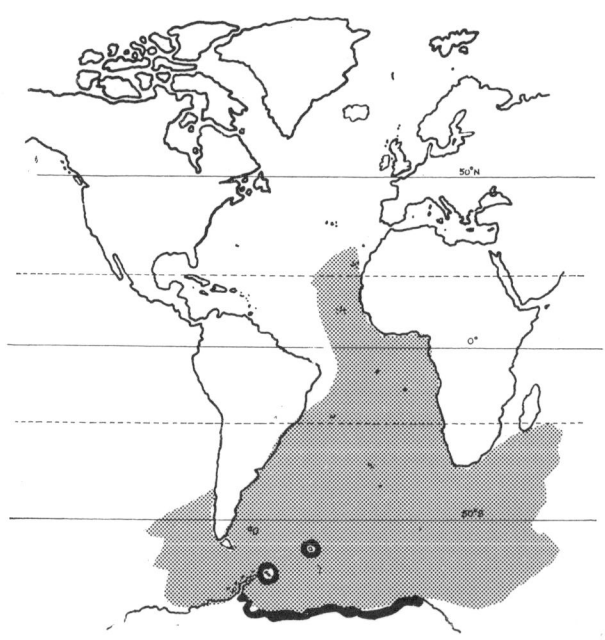

colouring, too, makes them extremely conspicuous and quite unmistakable.

The single, white egg is laid any time between November and May and breeding colonies exist on the Antarctic continent, in the South Shetlands, South Orkneys and South Georgia.

At sea, the pintado looks a decorative and harmless bird – a bird which, like the albatross and the southern cross, seamen welcome as indication of their arrival in the great oceans of the south. However, when pintados assemble, as they do from time to time, in southern harbours, they show themselves up in their true colours; greedy and vicious beyond belief, brooking no nonsense from any other creature in their insatiable appetite for edible flotsam of any description.

ANTARCTIC FULMAR

Fulmarus glacialoides

Wing span 42 inches.

Breeding on the coasts of Antarctica, this bird so nearly resembles the northern fulmar in appearance and habits, it seems likely that it is so closely related that it represents a geographical race of the species. Or rather tne other way round; that, somehow, the species originating in the southern seas has, sometime way back, found its way north and established itself in northern waters to develop along separate, though similar, lines.

The Antarctic fulmar, from records available, would appear to be slightly smaller than its northern counterpart and, in coloration, to be something between the light and dark phases of the northern fulmar. The southern bird is not polymorphic as the northern one, but this could be accounted for by the theory, held by some, that the temperature of the water at the time of breeding and in the vicinity of the breeding area affects the future colour of the young bird. The breeding sites of northern fulmars extend from well inside the Arctic circle to temperate northern Europe, whereas the breeding sites of the Antarctic fulmar are all distributed around the main Antarctic continent where the summer water temperature is constantly close to freezing point.

FULMAR

Fulmarus glacialis

Wing span 45 inches.

To the uninitiated, the fulmar could easily be mistaken for a gull. Though the bird is polymorphic, phases of colouring varying from quite dark sooty grey to almost white, it is the light birds – the most gull-like in colouring – which breed in the most populated portions of the birds' range and the average layman could – and does – just dismiss it as another 'seagull'.

In fact, there are several vital features which immediately distinguish this, the most frequently observed of the whole order of tubenoses in northern latitudes, from any gull. First, there is the distinctive tubenose bill; stubby and yellow with the nostrils arranged as two distinct tubes along its upper surface. Then the short, fat neck which gives the bird a dumpy, round-headed look. The wings, which are pearl-grey above with a light patch at the base of the primaries, are straight and rigid – not cranked like a gull's. Even the white of the light phase fulmar is not the 'white' white of a gull, but creamy, particularly about the head and breast.

Except when breeding, this little 'albatross' – some think of it that way – is a strictly pelagic bird, spending its life on the high seas, well out of sight of land.

Man, the world's most devastating predator, has, in the case of the fulmar, been responsible for an enormous increase in the numbers and range of the species in the last hundred years. The bird feeds fundamentally on plankton, squids, jellyfish, crustacea and so on, but modern commercial methods of fishing with attendant gutting and cleaning at sea

BIRDS OF THE ATLANTIC OCEAN

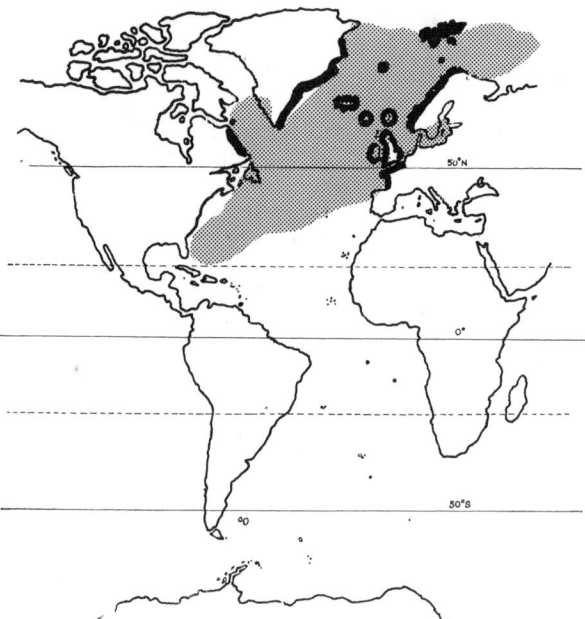

has attracted enormous numbers of fulmars to the commoner fishing grounds; for the fulmar is a scavenger *par excellence*. Near places where food is readily available, the bird breeds and whereas, in 1877, there was only a single nesting colony in the British Isles, colonies now encircle Britain and some have been established in the Channel Islands and northern France. It is interesting to note that, on the American Atlantic seaboard, fulmars breed no farther south than northern Labrador.

As well as in temperate Europe, fulmars breed well inside the Arctic circle. Broadly speaking, the further north the birds breed, the darker their colour phase – probably there is a direct relationship with water temperature.

The fulmar lays one white egg – very rarely two. The nest is a sparsely lined scoop on a cliff ledge – usually towards the top of the cliff. Birds frequently breed in among colonies of gulls. The mastery of flight of the fulmar, dancing on the up-currents at the cliff face, has to be seen to be believed. Every component of the bird's body – head, tail, individual wing feathers, legs and all – is called into play in an incredible display of airmanship.

There is a long incubation period – fifty-three days – and the young bird is forty-eight further days at the nest before it is finally deserted by its parents. It then finds its own way down to the water and off to sea.

Non-breeding birds disperse over wide areas of the Arctic and north Atlantic oceans, feeding at the fringes of the Gulf Stream and following fishing vessels wherever they go.

ANTARCTIC PETREL
Fulmarus (Thalassoica) antarcticus

Wing span 44 inches.

This petrel, which is dull brown above and white beneath, with a very broad and conspicuous white band across the wings, is a bird of the very far south. It is seldom seen north of 60°S., though it has been recorded as far north as Cape Horn and in the vicinity of South Georgia.

Along the edge of the Antarctic ice, the bird is fairly common and is to be seen in the same sort of habitat as the all-white snow petrel; on the edge of the oceanic pack ice.

Not much is known about the breeding grounds of the Antarctic petrel, but the ones which are known seem to be close to large bodies of high, glaciated land. Nests which have been found are on steep slopes, crowded in large colonies, with the eggs laid on bare soil among clefts and gullies.

Mt. Biscoe, up to heights of more than 3,000 ft, has large numbers of the species, breeding from January onwards. It is believed that the bird nests on the South Shetlands as well as on the continent of Antarctica.

The birds are reported, out of the breeding season, to have been seen clustered in great numbers on bergs and iceflows; squatting rather than standing, their white underparts matching the snow so that only their brown upper parts remained visible.

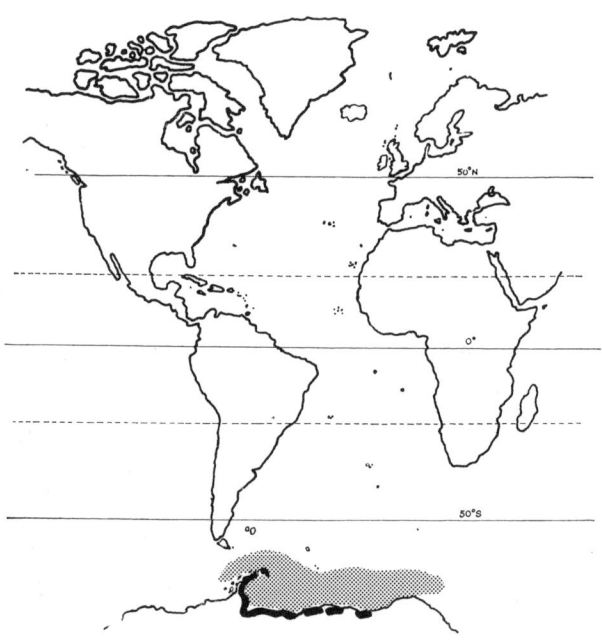

Snow Petrel

BIRDS OF THE ATLANTIC OCEAN

SNOW PETREL
Pagodroma nivea

Wing span 24 inches.

This beautiful petrel of the Antarctic is entirely white except for its black bill, blue-grey legs and feet, and a black spot in front of and just above the eye. It is not surprising, therefore, to find that it is a bird which is inseparable in thought and in fact from ice and snow. Ornithologists have described the bird variously, but usually colourfully: 'It is so white that it forms a contrast with the snow', and 'a large-eyed wraith gliding through the snow blown before williwaws from the upper slopes of the mountains'.

Snow petrels do not seem to nest in definite, recognisable colonies, but select individual ledges on peaks and cliffs in inaccessible places. The single white egg is laid in early December. While incubating, the bird sits very close and is extremely fearless. If picked up off the nest, it ejects a yellowy oily fluid in the fashion of all petrels.

They nest, frequently great distances from the sea, on South Georgia, South Orkneys and the Antarctic mainland. Their range is circum-polar, but they seldom wander as far north as Cape Horn.

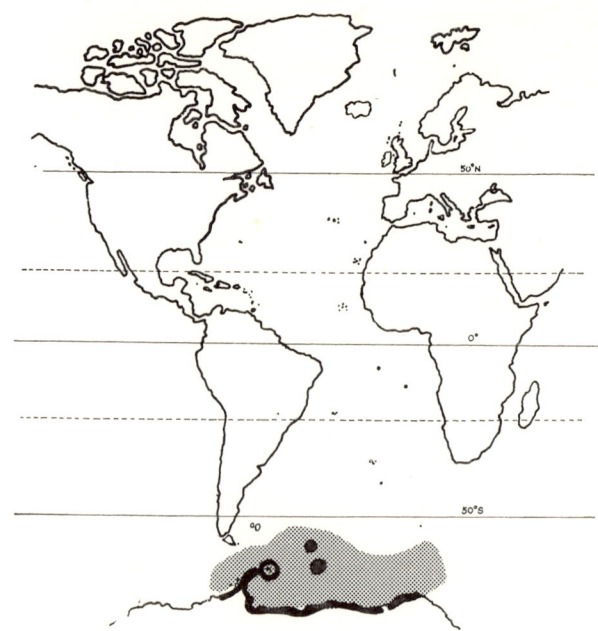

The bird has an incongruously raucous voice, quite out of keeping with its immaculate appearance. A loud *'caw'* has been described as well as 'a noisy twittering' and 'a remarkable half-whistling, half-shrieking'.

Sub-family *Pachyptilinae* – prions

BLUE PETREL
Halobaena caerulea

Wing span 26 inches.

The blue petrel is normally included in sub-family *pachyptilinae*, although it is actually something between a fulmar and a prion. It is blue-grey on the back and white beneath. The chest is grey. The head is a dark brownish-grey on the crown and nape, and the forehead is whitish. There is no pronounced white stripe on the back, which distinguishes this species from other prions. It is larger, with distinctly longer wings, and the tip of the tail is white whereas it is black in all other prions.

Although the bird has an enormous range, having been reported from all southern oceans, it does not appear to be very common. There are very few specimens in the museums of the world. It is frequently reported in company with prions from which

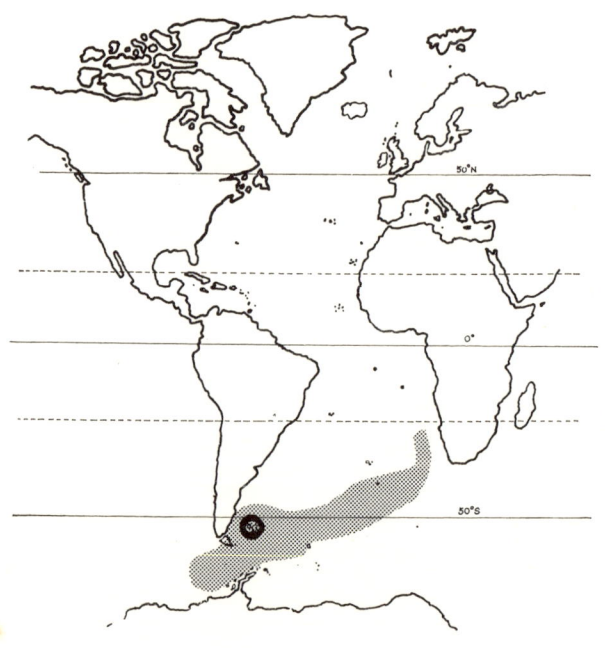

it is difficult to distinguish unless close observation is possible.

Blue petrels nest in the Falkland Islands, where they lay their single egg, which varies considerably in size and shape, in burrows dug in soft, dry ground. Like most of their family, they are nocturnal at the nesting site where they swarm noisily, making an incessant pigeon-like cooing. Eggs are laid in September, the young appear in November and are not fully fledged until February.

FAIRY PRION

Pachyptila turtur

Wing span 16 inches.

This is the smallest, bluest and palest of the prions or whale-birds. One of its unofficial names – a name given to it by the sailors of old – is snow bird. This name is not indicative of its habitat, but is descriptive, in that flocks of fairy prions resemble flurries of snow.

The birds are known to nest in the Pacific, but no known nesting site exists in the Atlantic. Birds have, however, been recovered from extreme South America and from the vicinity of the Cape of Good Hope, so they probably wander to the Atlantic outside the breeding season.

Nocturnal birds at the nesting site, like most *Procellariidae,* they are known to breed in southern Australia and New Zealand and reports have frequently come in of sightings of flocks estimated to contain perhaps millions of these birds in the seas around.

Whale-birds are so called because of the serrated edge of the upper mandible. The bird is capable of inflating a pouch in its throat into which it takes a quantity of sea water when feeding. The pouch is then deflated, blowing the water out and leaving the microscopic sea creatures, on which the bird lives, caught in the fine comb-like sieve of the beak. This structure is likened to the whale's baleen and has a similar function.

THIN-BILLED PRION

(Syn.: slender-billed whale-bird)

Pachyptila belcheri

Wing span 20 inches.

This is a smaller bird than the two which follow, but is very similar in appearance. So alike are all the prions, in fact, that they cannot normally be individually identified on the wing. In the hand, however, the thin-billed prion is immediately distinguished by the slender structure of the bill.

The general colour of the back, sides of neck and breast is blue-grey. The throat and belly are white or white, delicately tinged with pale blue. The crown is slightly darker than the rest of the back of the bird and there is a small black line around the eyelids, running thence backwards a short way on the side of the face. Above this is a white eye-stripe. A dark line

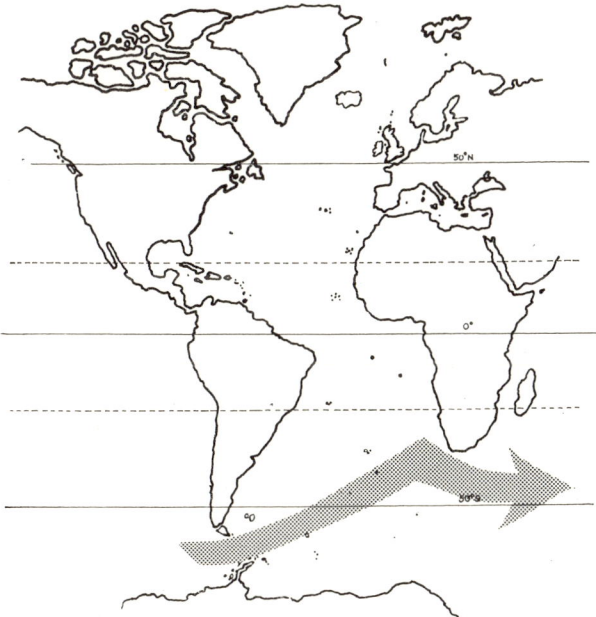

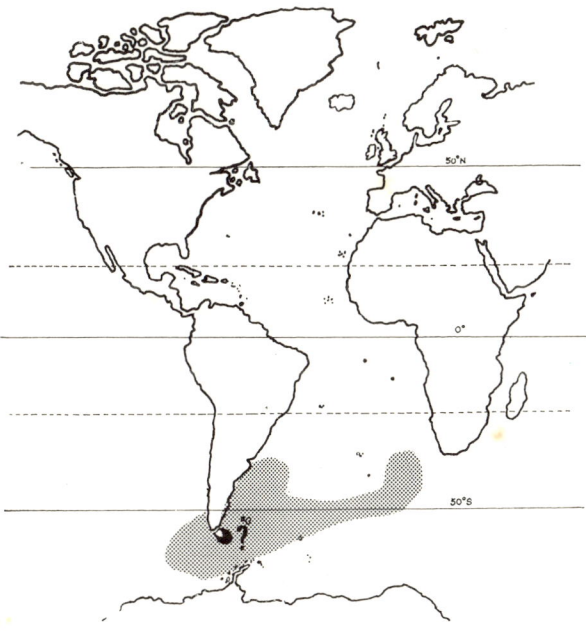

BIRDS OF THE ATLANTIC OCEAN

crosses the back in Vee form, its extremities being at the wing tips, the apex of the Vee pointing to, and almost joining, the black tail.

It is not at all certain where the thin-billed prion nests, though the most probable Atlantic nesting sites are on Staten Island and parts of Tierra del Fuego.

DOVE PRION

(Syn.: Antarctic whale-bird)

Pachyptila desolata

Wing span 21 inches.

Prions or whale-birds are seen in many parts of the oceans of the far south, usually in enormous, quite uncountable flocks. Observers generally agree that the remarkable thing about these flocks is that they appear and disappear as if by magic. The birds fly swiftly and near the surface of the sea, feeding in dense flocks in the high plankton areas. They wheel and turn close to water in rapid restless flight, apparently appearing and disappearing out of nowhere. Their disappearing act is explained when the observer on the deck knows that first their blue backs merge completely with the ocean, then their lighter undersides flash out in contrast while the birds turn away. If the birds are above, the white undersides are less distinguishable against the pale Antarctic sky than the blue backs.

1. Dove Prion.   2. Schlegel's Petrel.
3. Dove Prion (plan view of head).
4. Great-winged Petrel.   5. Herald Petrel.   6. Kerguelen Petrel.
7. Soft-plumaged Petrel.   8. Broad-billed Prion.
9. Broad-billed Prion (plan view of head).

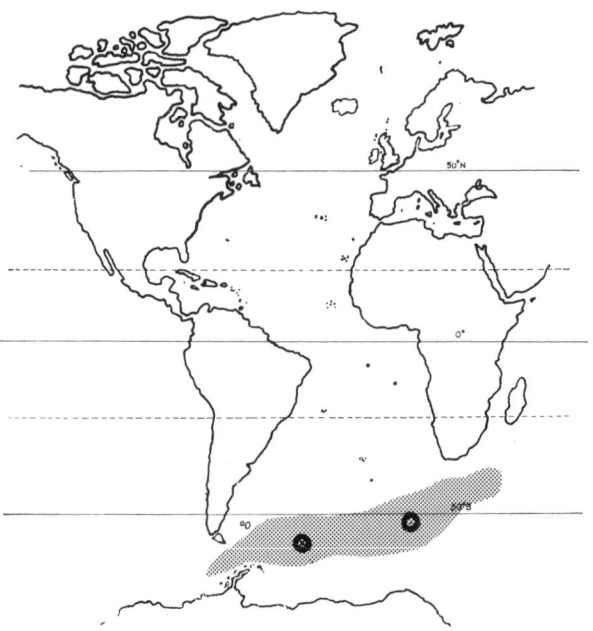

Naval aircraft in the Second World War were painted blue-grey above and very pale grey beneath. This camouflage, the most effective over the ocean, is said to have been copied from the prion.

In the Atlantic, the dove prions breed at South Georgia and at Bouvet Island. They nest in burrows, laying one white egg and, though prey to murderous destruction by man-introduced rats and though frequently caught by skuas at the entrances to their burrows should they venture in or out when it is not quite dark, they still manage to reproduce and survive in vast numbers.

In South Georgia, the breeding birds come in from the ocean in October and lay their eggs in mid-November. The young birds hatch during January and February. They do not eventually leave their burrows until May, after the ground is already well covered in snow.

The noise the birds make at their breeding site has been variously described as 'twittering', 'groaning' and 'cooing like a turtle dove'. All, however, agree that the noise issuing from underground, as

well as from the air early in the breeding season, is very considerable.

BROAD-BILLED PRION

(Syn.: broad-billed whale-bird)

Pachyptila vittata

Wing span 21 inches.

In flight, this bird is difficult to distinguish from any of the other prions. The size and colour are very similar to the two preceeding species. At close quarters, however, the bill is immediately diagnostic. It is broad, almost frog-like, and the pouch beneath is accentuated; grotesque. Close examination of the bill shows that the baleen-like filter mechanism on the upper mandible is the most developed of all the prions.

Having the most northerly range of Atlantic prions, this bird nests in the Tristan da Cunha group and at Gough Island. One white egg, about the size of a pigeon's egg, is laid in a burrow in September. The young do not leave the burrows until late May or even June.

The birds, when not at the nesting sites, range far over the southern ocean in the Atlantic as far north as sub-tropical regions.

In other ways, this species so closely resembles *P. belcheri* and *P. desolata* that further description would merely be repetition.

GREAT-WINGED PETREL

Pterodroma macroptera

Wing span 42 inches.

The great-winged petrel ranges over all southern oceans between latitudes 30°S. and 50°S. Birds of the Atlantic race of the species differ slightly from those of the Pacific. Typical great-winged petrels from New Zealand and other Pacific islands are black with grey faces. The Atlantic bird is uniformly black, or rather dark sooty brown, with a suspicion of grey only at the base of the bill and on the throat. It is also slightly smaller than the Pacific bird.

As the name implies, this bird has very long narrow wings. It has been described as resembling a large swift. Large numbers of great-winged petrels nest on Nightingale Island in the Tristan da Cunha group. They also probably nest at Gough Island. The nest is in a burrow in soft earth; a burrow only about a yard long. Nests have been found in suitable soil as much as 1,000 feet above sea level.

The birds come in to their burrows from the ocean as early as March, but do not lay their single eggs until July or August. The incubation period is about a month, but the young do not finally leave their burrows before January.

In North Island, New Zealand, the Maoris take the young, which are fat and tasty, for food, calling them 'mutton birds'. In Tristan the birds are known as 'black eaglets'.

The great-winged petrel has an enormous feeding range. During daylight hours, even in the breeding

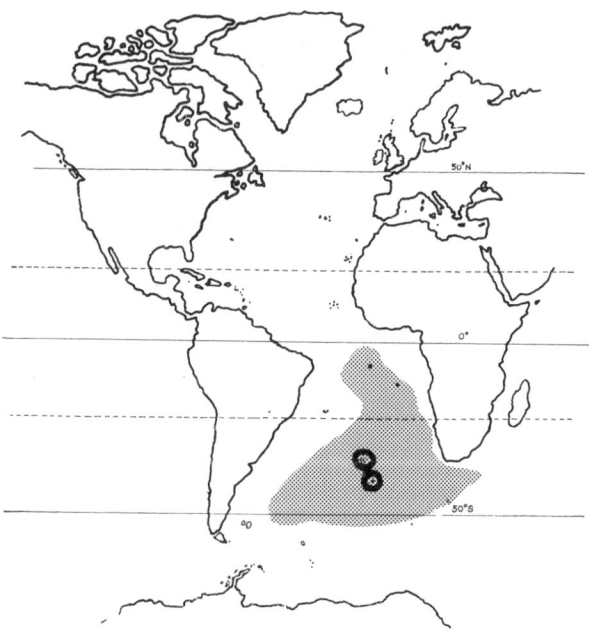

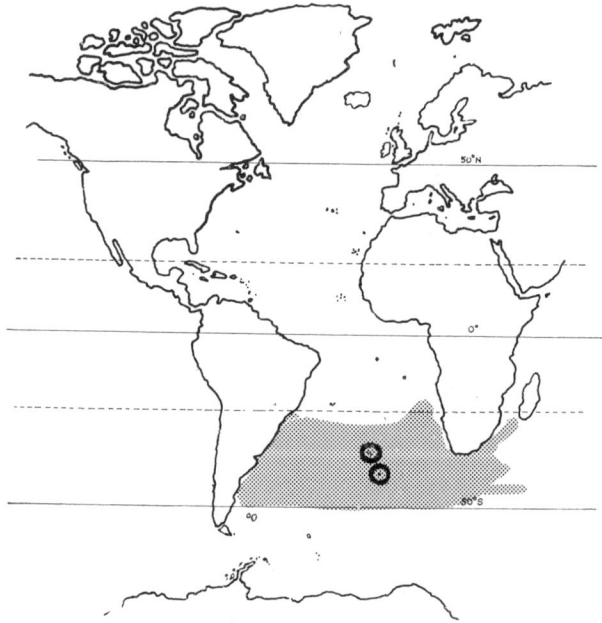

season, it is seldom seen within fifty miles of the land. Its diet consists exclusively of truly pelagic marine creatures.

eating and thriving industries exist on its breeding grounds. Today the annual harvest of young is regulated to maintain the annual yield.

SCHLEGEL'S PETREL

(Syn.: Atlantic petrel)

Pterodroma incerta

Wing span 36 inches.

This is a handsome and extremely abundant petrel, which may be seen right across the Atlantic from the Cape of Good Hope to Brazil and between the tropic of Capricorn and latitude 50°S. In spite of the birds' apparent abundance, very little is known about it. There is, however, evidence that Schlegel's petrel breeds in the Tristan da Cunha group and that, like most others of its family, it lays one white egg in a burrow in a hillside.

Schlegel's petrel – the Atlantic race of a super species which is circum-global in distribution – is a rich brown on the back, darkening to sooty-brown at extremities, white beneath except for a brown throat and upper chest, and brown beneath the rather long, wedge-shaped tail. There is a broad, not very distinct eye-stripe running under the eye. The legs and feet are orangy flesh-colour; the extremities of the toes brown.

This is one of several species known to sailors and islanders as 'mutton birds'. They make very good

SOFT-PLUMAGED PETREL

Pterodroma mollis

Wing span 35 inches.

The soft-plumaged petrel is a bird of both North and South Atlantic. In the South Atlantic it is an abundant species, whereas in the North Atlantic a distinct race of the same species is rather rare. The bird is slaty-grey on the back with blackish-brown wing tips. The head is slightly darker than the back; the forehead and cheeks are white or mottled white; the chin grey and the belly white. There is a black eye-stripe below the eye. The bill is black. The legs are flesh-coloured except for the outer two-thirds of the feet which are deep brown.

The North Atlantic race breeds at Madeira and the Cape Verde Islands; laying in June or July. The South Atlantic race breeds at Tristan da Cunha and Gough Island. On Nightingale Island and Inaccessible Island in the Tristan group, the single white eggs are laid early in November in burrows which are, in places, under the floor of wooded groves where noddies nest in the trees.

In the South Atlantic, the birds are essentially pelagic and are sometimes encountered in large flocks many hundreds of miles from their known

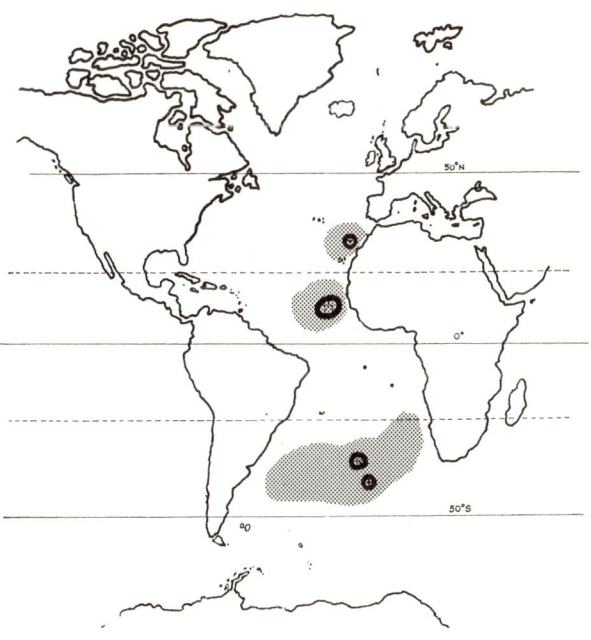

nesting sites. On the other hand, in the North Atlantic, there seem to be very few records of sightings of these birds in places far from where they breed.

KERGUELEN PETREL
Pterodroma brevirostris

Wing span 24 inches.

This small, slaty-grey petrel which breeds at Kerguelen Island, outside the geographic limits of this work, was, for some time, said to breed at Tristan da Cunha. This theory was based on one specimen at the British Museum which was obtained from Tristan. It is, of course, possible that the bird was accidentally storm-blown there and this seems most likely as the normal range of the species is confined to high Antarctic latitudes. In fact, there seems to be no other record of the bird being sighted north of latitude 65°S.

It is probable, as the bird is often reported from high latitudes in the Atlantic sector, that it nests at places other than Kerguelen Island. The islands at the northern approaches to the Weddell Sea are possible.

At Kerguelen, the petrel lays its egg in a rather deep, damp burrow; the dampness being apparently the result of thawing ice in the soil. Laying takes place early in October. The young are not fledged by mid-December. Little more is known about them.

HERALD PETREL
(Syn.: South Trinidad petrel)
Pterodroma arminjoniana

Wing span 39 inches.

The nomenclature of this bird is an interesting illustration of the welcome simplification of ornithological classification which has taken place in recent years. In *Birds of the Ocean* (Alexander, 1928) the herald petrel is described as *Pterodroma heraldica*, a bird of the warmer parts of the Pacific. In the same book, the name Kermadec petrel, *Pterodroma neglecta*, is given to a very similar bird associated with Kermadec Island and other east Pacific Islands. The Trinidad petrel, which is the bird concerned with this work, was specified as *P. arminjoniana*. Murphy, in *Oceanic Birds of South America* (1936), separated them similarly, though he did not mention *P. heraldica* as it was not concerned with his area. Fisher and Lockley in *Sea Birds* (1954) report *P. neglecta* as having been storm driven to England; this supposedly from the Pacific.

The modern acceptance of the fact that all these birds are conspecific and the naming of the super species 'herald' is obviously wise and, if correct, might account for the arrival of *P. neglecta* in England, for birds from the tropical zone of the Atlantic have frequently been blown further afield than this.

Confusion has probably arisen in the past as the herald petrel is a bird of many garbs. Individual

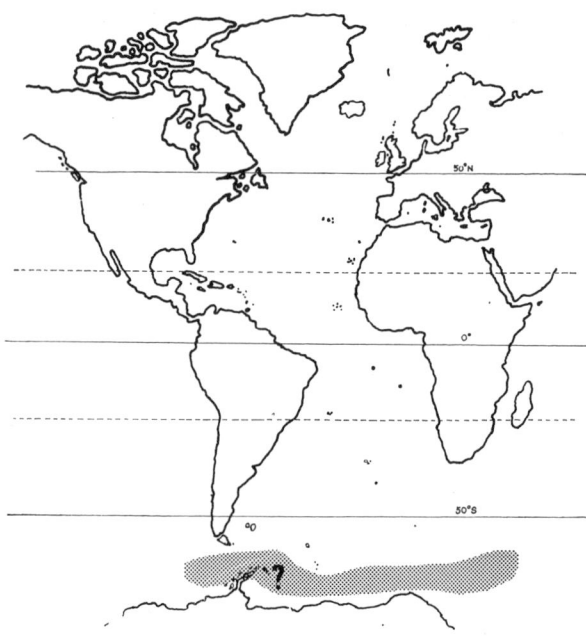
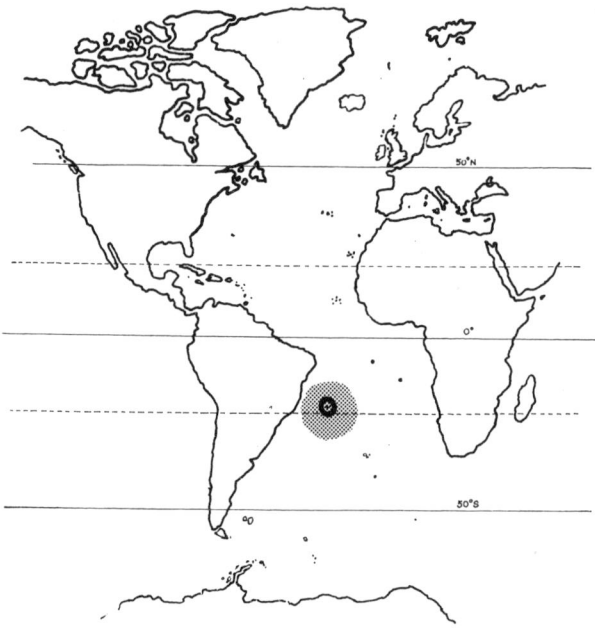

colour form, moreover, does not necessarily interbreed with individual colour form. The light birds are ashy-grey and brown, mottled with white above, and white beneath except for an ashy-brown band across the neck. The dark birds are nearly entirely black or ashy-brown, more or less mottled with white. There is also a record of a white bird, flecked with black. The bill is always black, but legs vary from partly flesh-colour to entirely black.

This race is a native of South Trinidad Island. Breeding continues throughout the year. Birds do not normally seem to wander more than about 300 miles from their breeding ground, though there have been accidental reports from the North Atlantic, most of which have been directly attributable to the work of tropical storms.

CAPPED PETREL

(Syns: black-capped petrel, West Indian petrel, diablotin)

Pterodroma hasitata

Wing span 38 inches.

We have just – see *P. arminjoniana* – examined the case of the modern acceptance of several obviously related species as one super species. In the case of *P. hasitata* and *P. cahow*, however, we have an example of two very rare and little-known birds which in the past have always been assumed to be

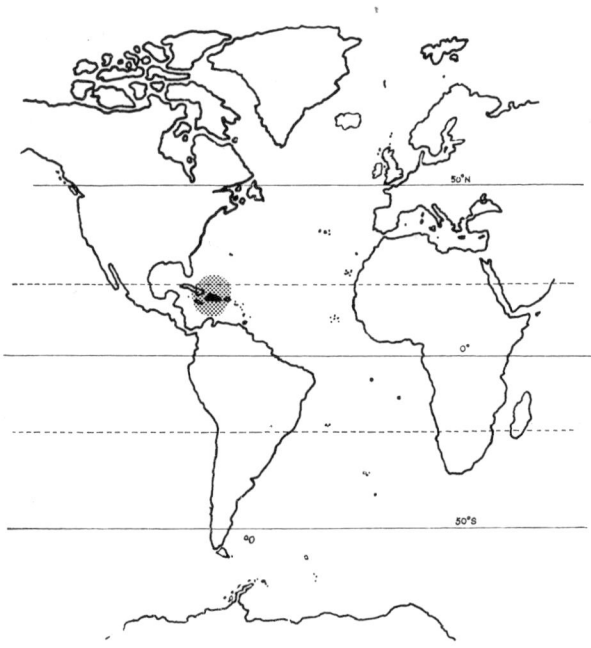

races of the same species, but are now accepted as two separate species. The ways of scientists are indeed difficult for the mere layman to understand. Inspection of the skeletons of the two birds reveal that they are identical in shape, though a different size. The colouring of the two birds is slightly different, but their voices are the same. Their chosen nesting sites are very different. But the north European man and the pigmy are a different colour, are different sizes, have different shaped skeletons and certainly 'nest' in different sites; yet no one doubts that they are merely race variations of the species *H. sapiens*.

For many years, the existence of the capped petrel has been known and there are records of breeding colonies in Jamaica and Haiti, though these were assumed to have disappeared or become practically extinguished by the predations of the mongoose and the rat. However, reports of the bird at sea and the occasional recovery of storm-blown specimens showed, up to the present time, that the bird still survived; but no-one knew where.

Space does not permit a full history in this work, but in 1961 David Wingate was enabled to make a search of Dominica and the Republic of Haiti and rediscovered at least one successful nesting site. At least eleven colonies were discovered, in inaccessible, forested cliffs up to 7,800 ft above sea level on the Massif de la Selle in the centre of Haiti; twelve miles from the nearest sea. He estimated that there were at least 4,000 breeding birds.

The bird is typical of the sub-family concerned; straight winged, bulkier than a shearwater, with its legs situated not as far back as a true shearwater's. It is sooty-grey-brown on the back and wings, has a very marked black cap, a white forehead, nape, rump and belly. The legs are pale pink except for the terminal two thirds of the feet, which are black.

The voice varies from a sharp clicking noise to a long drawn out *'ooow-uk'*; sometimes, Wingate says, there are 'yelps like a hurt puppy'.

The breeding season is from November to May.

CAHOW

(Syn.: Bermuda petrel)

Pterodroma cahow

Wing span 35 inches.

Late in the 15th century, the early British settlers in Bermuda described a bird which lived in the islands, nesting in burrows in enormous numbers wherever the soil permitted. They called it the cahow. The bird, which was known to be a petrel of sorts, was found to be good to eat, and so was the single egg it laid. In about 1600, a grave shortage of food occurred in the Bermudas and the settlers turned more and more to eating the succulent cahow. From December onwards, when the birds came in to their nests, they were very easy to take. They were tame, the burrows were shallow and in soft soil. Great was the destruction of the gentle creatures.

In 1601, the Governor issued an edict declaring the 'spoiling of the cahowe' illegal. But he was too late; or so it seemed. For more than three hundred years, it was assumed that the Bermuda cahow was extinct.

In 1906 a bird was picked up dead on Castle Island, Bermuda, which was not immediately identified, but was thought, possibly, to be a capped petrel from the Caribbean. In 1916 another was found and people began to wonder. This bird seemed, impossibly, to tie up with the 16th/17th-century description of the bird called cahow. In 1931, a bird struck St David's Light and was picked up and definitely identified as the cahow. In 1944, one hit a telegraph pole at St George's and was also positively identified as a cahow. But none nested on the inhabited islands of Bermuda; whence, then, did they come?

In 1951, a search party was organised by Robert Murphy of the New York Natural History Museum and it was Louis Mowbray, the present curator of the Bermuda Aquarium, who solved the mystery; finding the birds – very few of them – nesting in rocky crevices on the tiny off-shore islands at the north-eastern end of Bermuda.

In the years 1965, '66 and '67 there were, respectively, twenty, twenty-one and twenty-two established breeding pairs. They successfully reared eight, six and eight young between them. Since 1957 there has been a desperately low and falling productivity rate and David Wingate, who has especial care of their protection, estimates that there are probably not more than about eighty birds of the species in the world.

The white-tailed tropic bird – Bermuda's most colourful and favourite breeder – has, in the past, used the same rock crevices as the cahow has now been driven to using. Tropic birds came in to nest after the young cahows were hatched, and promptly killed the fat fluffy creatures they found already in residence. To overcome this, Mowbray and Wingate, between them, devised stone or wooden baffles, not unlike the mud baffles nuthatches make at the entrances to their holes. Thus the tropic bird, whose thoracic measurement is greater than that of the cahow, has been effectively excluded.

But, since 1957, although the cahow population has risen, productivity has declined. It has now been established that this decline is due to D.D.T. poisoning. This new hazard is most alarming when it is remembered that the bird's sole source of food is oceanic plankton. It means that mankind in his criminal folly is thus not only seriously reducing the population of many land birds but, by polluting the oceanic food chain, is now threatening the very existence of all sea birds. If the present decline in productivity continues, reproduction of *P. cahow* will fail completely by 1978. It seems we can only pray for a miracle or – more positively – for timely international legislation banning the use of D.D.T.

Like the capped petrel, only smaller, and with the black cap merging into the dark back so that there is no white nape, the cahow appears to spend its life within a few hundred miles of Bermuda, fishing in the Gulf Stream. There is, so far, no record of the bird being positively identified at sea.

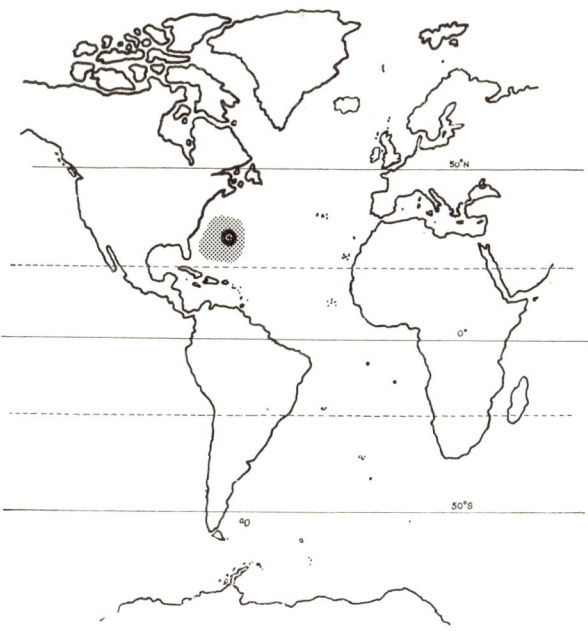

BULWER'S PETREL

Bulweria bulwerii

Wing span 24 inches.

A native of the Azores, Madeira, the Canary and Cape Verde Islands, this small dark petrel could almost be mistaken for a storm petrel. There are, however, essential differences. The head and black

BIRDS OF THE ATLANTIC OCEAN

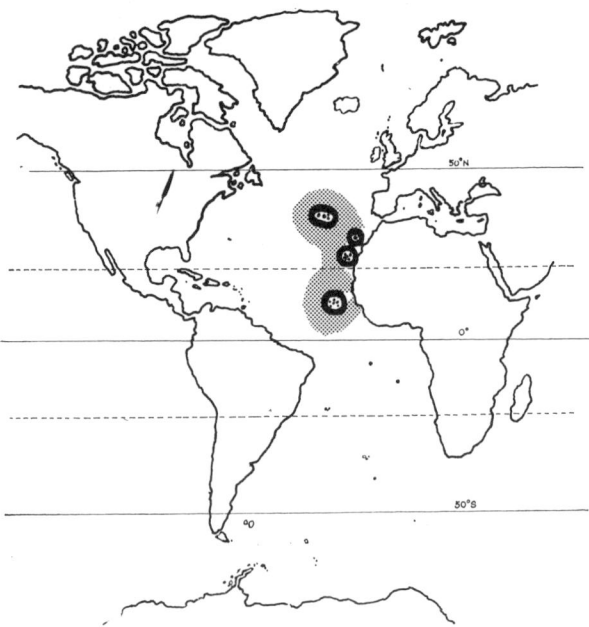

1. Manx Shearwater. 2. Cory's Shearwater. 3. Pediunker.
4. Little Shearwater. 5. Sooty Shearwater. 6. Shoemaker.
7. Bulwer's Petrel. 8. Capped Petrel.

bill, in particular, are long and shearwater-like in comparison with the round head of the storm petrel. The tail is long and wedge-shaped; not square or forked as the storm petrel's. The flesh-coloured and black legs and feet are shorter in relation to the size of the bird.

Early in the year – at courtship time – the birds come in from the wide ocean and, like other members of their family, indulge in a characteristic circling flight. Unlike others, however, the Bulwer's petrel's courtship flight is silent.

The single egg is laid in a burrow in May or June.

Incubation and fledging periods are long, as with all the family. The chicks of storm petrels are born blind and feeble. Those of Bulwer's petrel are born fluffy and active and with their eyes open.

Sub-family *Procellariinae* – petrels and shearwaters

SHOEMAKER

(Syns: white-chinned petrel, Cape hen)

Procellaria aequinoctialis

Wing span 55 inches.

'... and I sing as I cobble this doleful lay'. So sings the cobbler of *Chu Chin Chow,* and it is said that the shoemaker is so called because he sits at home and sings. The lay, however, is not at all doleful. The bird has been described as being the noisiest of all the family. It chatters and grunts and has a 'high trill like a water whistle'. All this chatter goes on at the nesting burrows and the bird is silent at sea except when captured or in distress.

The shoemaker, the first in the order of the true shearwaters, is sooty-black with a yellow or greenish-yellow bill and black legs and feet. The chin varies enormously from bird to bird. Some have no white at all on their chins, others have a white spot, others have an entirely white chin and throat and even, possibly, a white spot or two on their bellies.

Shoemakers can be seen over a wide area of the South Atlantic, from 30°S. to 60°S. They never go further south than the fringes of the pack ice. Their Atlantic breeding stations are at South Georgia

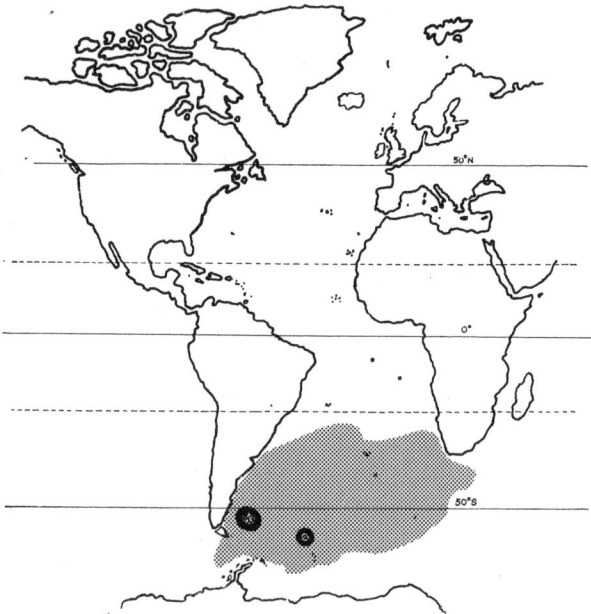
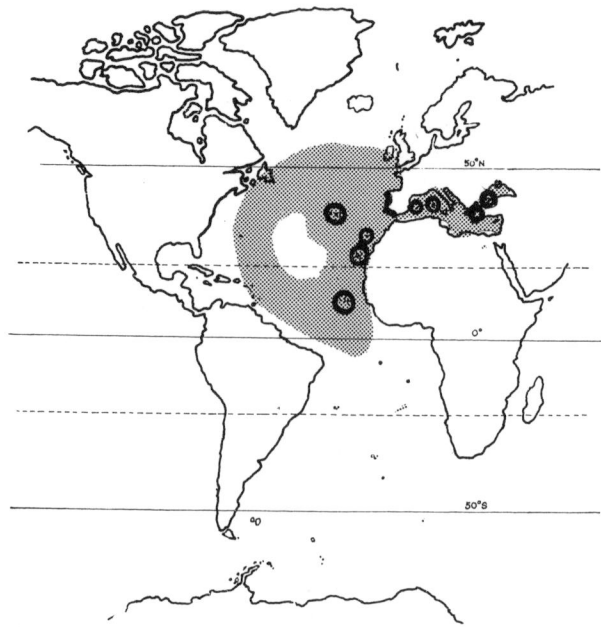

and the Falklands where they inhabit burrows in thickly populated warrens, usually on lee slopes. They come ashore to burrow and begin courtship in October. The single white egg – sometimes spotted and stained – is laid in November. Incubation is fifty to sixty days and the young are finally abandoned in April, making their own way down to the sea in May.

Being a large bird, the shoemaker has little fear of skuas and other predators so its movements at the nesting site are less nocturnal than others of the petrel family. Birds frequently sit about sunning themselves in the vicinity of the burrows.

To return to the bird's propensity for chatter, it is said that it is easy to tell if a burrow is occupied as any caller is greeted with a flood of comment from below the ground!

CORY'S SHEARWATER

(Syns: cinerous shearwater, Mediterranean shearwater, North Atlantic shearwater)

Procellaria diomedea

Wing span 45 inches.

This is the largest North Atlantic shearwater. It breeds on islands off the Atlantic coast of Spain and Portugal, in the Azores, in the Desertas and Salvages of the Madeira group, in the Canaries, the Cape Verde Islands, throughout the Mediterranean, and even in the Black Sea.

The bird is essentially pale brown on the back and white beneath, the various shades merging gradually with each other. It has a large, yellowish-brown bill.

Birds of this sub-family are long and torpedo-like with long, straight, narrow wings. They are masters of flapless flight, skimming close to the surface of the water, with little apparent effort, on long narrow wings. Their short legs are situated very far aft.

Cory's shearwaters do not, as a rule, nest in burrows. Being large birds they are less nocturnal than some of their relations and they seem to choose caves and rock crannies as nesting sites where, frequently, they build pyramids of stone on which to lay their egg.

It is a curious thing that although enormous numbers of these shearwaters breed on the eastern side of the Atlantic (20,000 pairs have been counted on the Salvage Islands alone), they are not as frequently seen in British waters as Tristan great shearwaters, whose only breeding station is in the Tristan group in the South Atlantic.

The out of breeding season ocean circulation of *Procellariinae* seems to form a general pattern of clockwise movement; south from the north-eastern stations; north and west from the southern breeding stations; then eastward and south again. Off Bermuda, where Wingate has recently made some careful observations, enormous flocks of shearwaters – Cory's, Manx, Tristan great and sooty (the first two, presumably, being the non-breeding birds) – pass northward for days on end in May and June. Cory's shearwaters seem to concentrate off the north-east coast of America while the Tristan great shearwaters gather off the British Isles and north European coasts. What is certain is that birds of the sub-family never linger in warm water regions where, presumably, their preferred food is either not plentiful or not readily obtainable.

PEDIUNKER

(Syns: night-hawk, grey petrel, black-tailed petrel, Cape dove)

Procellaria cinerea

Wing span 44 inches.

The pediunker – a name given the bird by the inhabitants of Tristan da Cunha – is one of the commonest shearwaters in the lower South Atlantic latitudes. It has circum-global distribution south of the equator, but, in the Atlantic, breeds in the Tristan group and on Gough Island.

Uniformly grey on its back except for a brown tinge on the head and darker tail and wing tips, the bird has a white belly, dusky throat and chin, a dirty white bill with black horizontal stripes, dirty white legs and feet with yellowish webs. Under the tail is grey.

Pediunkers nest high on mountain slopes. On Gough Island, the burrows have been found 2,000 feet above sea level. The birds are entirely nocturnal at the nesting site. Islanders used to catch them for food by lighting bonfires in the vicinity of the nest. The birds would flutter around and some would eventually fling themselves to their deaths in the fire. This rather barbarous sounding method of catching petrels and shearwaters is still used in many parts of the world with other species. Laying dates vary, though it is thought birds probably first come back from sea to the burrows in September.

The incubation and fledging periods are not known for sure, but they are certainly very protracted.

When not breeding, pediunkers range over all southern oceans between latitudes 25°S. and 50°S. In places where cold currents thrust northward along continental shelves they even penetrate the tropics. The species is strictly pelagic and is never seen within sight of land except when breeding. The flight is described as a fast, graceful, dipping movement with long periods of gliding, but when the wings are flapped, the beat is very quick, almost duck-like.

Pediunkers feed on plankton and cephalopods like most petrels, but are also known to dive for fish, sometimes remaining submerged for several minutes.

TRISTAN GREAT SHEARWATER

(Syns: greater shearwater, hagdon)

Puffinus gravis

Wing span 43 inches.

The only known breeding place of this species is in the Tristan da Cunha group. Yet enormous numbers of Tristan great shearwaters annually invade the North Atlantic, travelling north-west across the

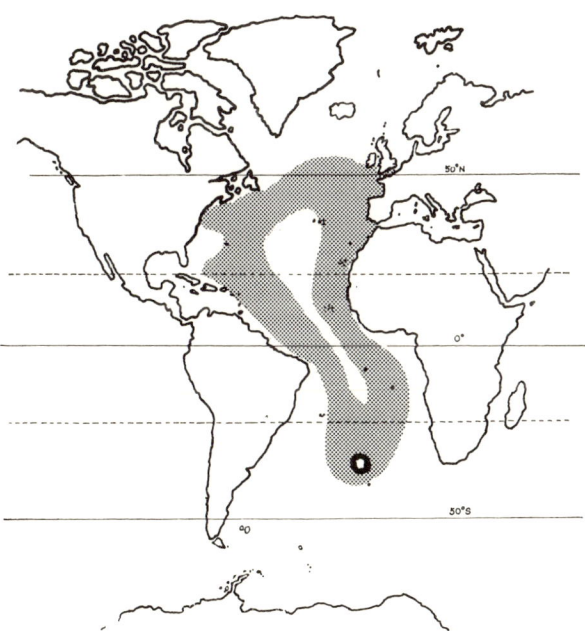

BIRDS OF THE ATLANTIC OCEAN

equator in the direction of Florida, thence north past Bermuda to the New England coast, eastward across the Atlantic to the approaches to the English Channel where they arrive in early July, and then gradually south again to reach their ocean outpost in time for the laying season, which seems to be at its height in November. It is amazing that a species with such limited breeding grounds – high hillsides on Nightingale and Inaccessible Islands – a species which produces only one young at a time, is so successful. In the past, great numbers have been taken for food by fishermen or inadvertantly caught on mackerel lines, yet year after year this vast horde of shearwaters moves clockwise round the waters of the Atlantic.

The Tristan great shearwater is very easily distinguishable. Much larger and even more torpedo-like than the Manx shearwater, slightly smaller than Cory's shearwater, it is browny-grey on the back and light beneath, but with a very distinct dark brown cap, a white rump and a rather square, dark brown tail. The cap and tail look black at any distance.

Like the pediunker, the bird frequently feeds on surface-swimming fish and is frequently seen in the vicinity of herring and mackerel shoals with other marine and avian predators. It is an efficient and sometimes spectacular diver.

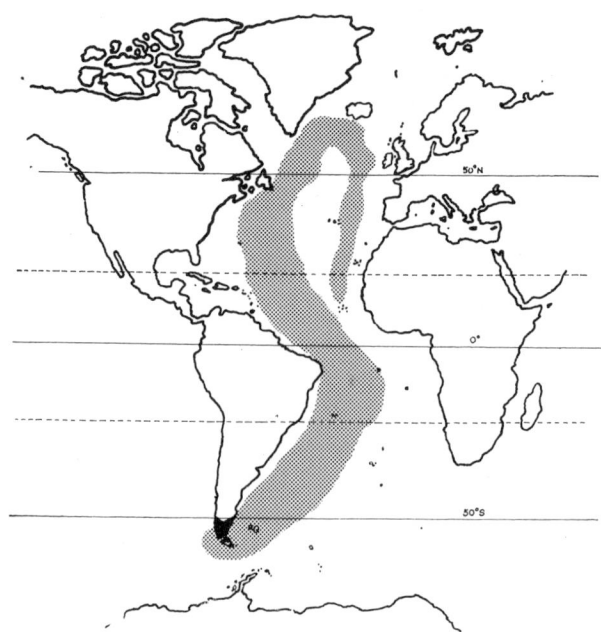

SOOTY SHEARWATER

(Syns: dusky shearwater, haglet)

Puffinus griseus

Wing span 42 inches.

This shearwater is a world-wide species, breeding in New Zealand and in South America and ranging north in both the Pacific and the Atlantic in vast numbers.

It is a dark, grey-brown bird with darker wing tips and tail. Under the wings it is white or grey and there is varying amount of white or grey marking in the vicinity of the eyes and cheeks. The legs are black with dark blue or purple webs. The bill is usually black.

This very typical shearwater – with graceful, gliding flight on long pointed wings, ever following the contours of the ocean – is seen in the Atlantic more frequently on the western side. However, numbers are reported each year from the eastern side, sometimes a few mixed up with large flocks of Tristan great shearwaters. From the western side come frequent reports of enormous concentrations of sooty shearwaters.

The Atlantic breeding birds nest in the region of the Straits of Magellan – on the mainland and on many of the islands in that region. The egg is white and elongated; laid in a chamber which is sometimes lightly lined, sometimes bare and wet, at the end of a yard-long burrow. The breeding season is from November to March.

In the north Atlantic summer, the birds stream north along the American coast, well out into the Atlantic, reaching as far north as Greenland and Iceland. Large numbers have been observed passing Bermuda, in sight of land, in the month of June.

The bird has a raucous voice which, at a distance and in chorus, is described as not unpleasant. But at the nesting site, particularly when the birds first come back, it is described as a terrifying noise like 'a choking cat'.

MANX SHEARWATER

(Syn.: common shearwater)

Puffinus puffinus

Wing span 32 inches.

The detailed studies of this species carried out by R. M. Lockley have confirmed much of the general life pattern of all *Procellariiformes,* previously

Tristan Great Shearwater

only guessed at from random observations of many species in many widely scattered localities. From 10,000 to 15,000 birds breed on the island of Skokholm off the Pembrokeshire coast and, for many years, have been kept under close observation throughout their long breeding season.

The Manx shearwater is as near black above and white beneath as makes no difference. There are brownish and greyish patches in the dark parts and grey mottling in the white parts, but the general impression is contrasting black and white. The slender, hooked bill with comparatively small independent nostril tubes is black. The legs are pink in front and black behind, and the feet are terminally black for the last third of their length. The webs are bluish-black.

The bird breeds on many islands in the northeastern Atlantic, particularly in the vicinity of the British Isles. It also breeds in the Azores, the Madeiras and off the Spanish and Portuguese coasts. Two distinct races breed in the Mediterranean – *mauretanicus* in the Balearics and *yelkouan* off Corsica, Sardinia, Malta and the Aegean Islands and in the Black Sea. There is a record of it breeding in Bermuda, but none breeds there now.

Birds of the race *yelkouan*, at certain times of the year, pass up and down between the Sea of Marmora and the Black Sea in enormous flocks. They are known locally in Istanbul as the 'Lost Souls of the Bosphorus' for they are apparently incessantly on the move not knowing where they are going or whence they came. Local legend has it that they are the souls of the sad concourse of Sultans' wives who have, throughout the ages, been strangled for infidelity or other marital misdemeanours, tied up in sacks and thrown into the Bosphorus. Their local official name is levantine shearwater; the Turkish name is 'Siyah gagali yelkuvan' and they have been recorded as far east as Cyprus.

In Skokholm, the birds arrive at their burrows in March. Their single eggs are laid in May. Incubation takes fifty-two to fifty-four days. Young birds are fully fledged sixty-two days after hatching, when they are deserted by their parents for a period of from eleven to fifteen days before they finally find their way down to the sea.

When not at the breeding site, they migrate many thousands of miles over the ocean. The pattern of migration would appear to be generally clockwise around the Atlantic Ocean. British breeding birds have been recovered off Buenos Aires.

A spectacular and oft-observed habit of the bird – one which is familiar to the countless mariners who use north European coastal waters – is that of collecting off the coast in vast floating crowds, or 'rafts' as they are called. One of the principal items in the Manx shearwater's diet is baby herring, for which birds dive and hunt, swimming under water with their wings.

LITTLE SHEARWATER

(Syns: pimblico, Audubon's shearwater, Madeiran little shearwater)

Puffinus assimilis

Wing span 24 inches.

Here we have another incident of the remarkable changes of nomenclature and accepted specification which has taken place in recent years. Little shearwater is now the accepted English name of the super species and *Puffinus assimilis* the accepted ornithological designation of the super species. *Puffinus assimilis* is, however, only one race of a considerable number, spread throughout the oceans of the world; a race which, incidentally, used to be known as the dusky shearwater. The Atlantic races of the species consist of the Audubon shearwater *(P. l'herminieri)*, which breeds in Bermuda and the West Indies, the Madeiran little shearwater *(P. baroli)*, which breeds in Madeira and the Azores, the Cape Verde Island race *(P. l'herminieri boydi)* and the Tristan and Gough Island race *(P. elegans)*.

Whatever the race, the birds of the species are very similar. Dark – nearly black – above, and white

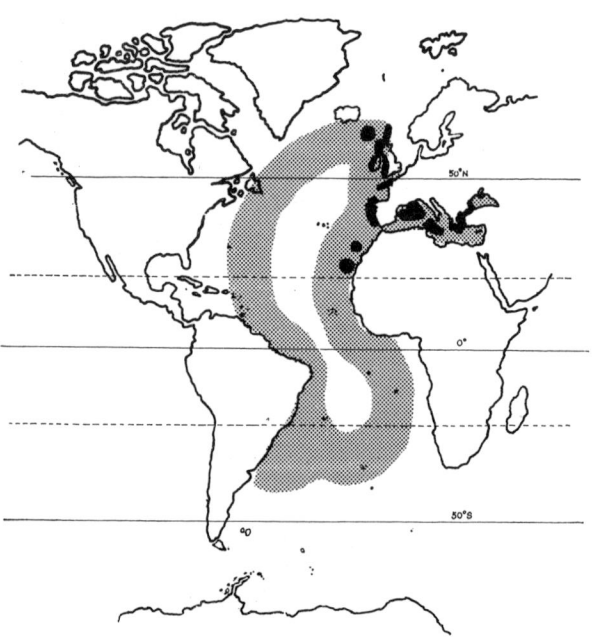

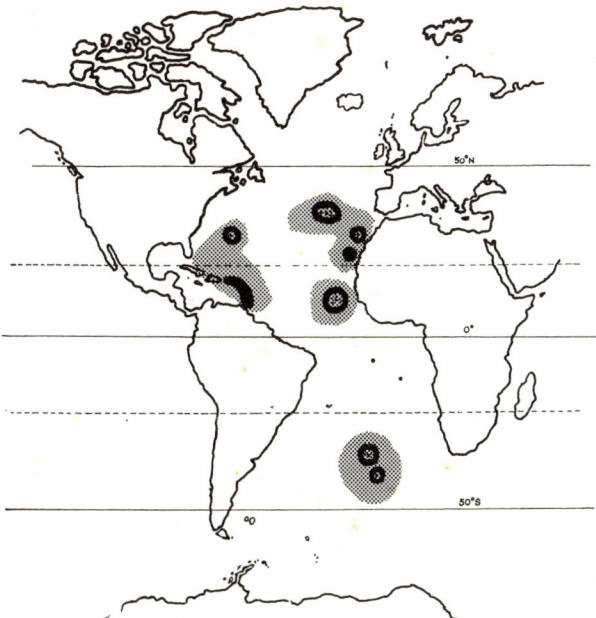

beneath. The bill is black, the feet slate-blue except for the outer toes which are black. It is a small, smart, noisy and very pugnacious bird.

Where the terrain permits, the nest is in the usual shearwater burrow, but in some small rocky islets an ordinary crevice in the rock is used. Laying takes place, of course, at different times in the year depending on latitude, but in the North Atlantic – Bermuda and the Azores – eggs are laid in March or April. The incubation period is fifty-three days and the fledging period seventy-two days.

There is no record of these little birds travelling great distances from their nesting site like some of the larger shearwaters, though they may well do this.

FAMILY *HYDROBATIDAE* – STORM PETRELS

The smallest members of the order, storm petrels have a special place in the hearts and myths of sailors. Not only are they the smallest tubenoses, they are the smallest of all sea birds, being not much larger than swallows. They have slender bills and very long legs for their size. Their flight is not as direct or as definite as that of their larger relatives, but erratic, almost moth-like. They are generally dark birds with longish wings for their size.

Myth – mariners' myth – surrounds them to a great extent. They are frequently known as Mother Carey's chickens, which name comes, in a roundabout fashion, from the Virgin Mary. Yet their appearance in the vicinity of a ship is said to forebode a storm. Their habit of trailing their legs and paddling the air with them when they are close to the sea's surface looks like a form of semi-airborne propulsion. It is thought that this habit was the origin of the name petrel, for they were said to try to walk on the water like St Peter.

BRITISH STORM PETREL

(Syn.: storm petrel)

Hydrobates pelagicus

Wing span 12 inches.

The smallest of the seven Atlantic storm petrels, it habitually follows in the wake of ships, dodging from side to side with a hesitant, fluttering flight. At night storm petrels frequently follow up the line of the logline, attracted, presumably, by the reflected glow of the overtaking light.

The bird is black, or nearly black, except for a whitish line across the top of the wings, and a brilliant patch on its rump. When seen in a ship's lights at night, it is extraordinarily reminiscent of a house martin. It is distinguished from its rather larger relatives, the Madeiran and Leach's petrel, by its square, not forked, tail, and from Wilson's storm petrel by its shorter legs and black feet.

It breeds in Iceland, Norway, the British Isles, Brittany, and the Mediterranean as far east as Malta. The egg is laid in May or slightly earlier according to location. The incubation period is

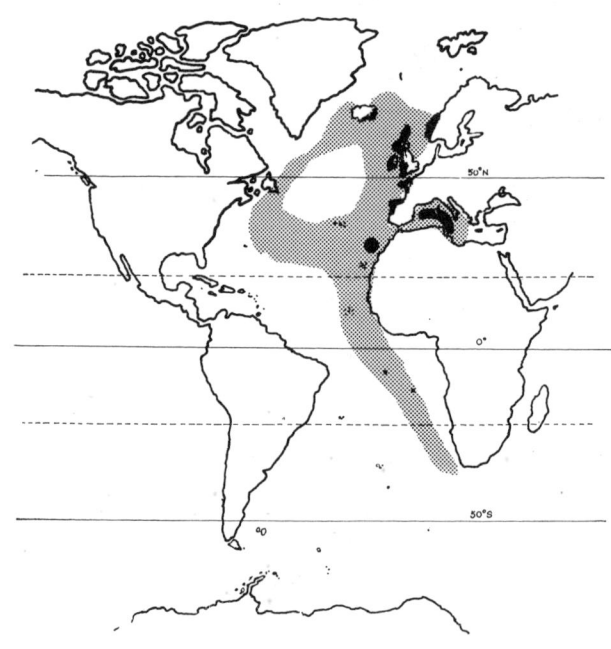

Leach's Storm Petrel

thirty-eight days and the fledging period sixty-one days. The nest is not, however, in an earth burrow, but in a rock crevice or under loose stones. The bird is completely nocturnal in nesting habits.

Outside the breeding season, British storm petrels keep mostly to the eastern side of the North Atlantic or to the Mediterranean, but they have been recorded on the North American coast and as far south as the Cape of Good Hope.

MADEIRAN STORM PETREL

Oceanodroma castro

Wing span 18 inches.

In spite of its name, the Madeiran storm petrel is a Pacific as well as an Atlantic bird. It is larger than the British storm petrel and has a slightly forked tail. The wings, head and tail are black, the wing coverts dark brown and there is the distinctive white band across the rump which extends to the flanks and under tail coverts. The bill is black and so are the legs.

In the Atlantic, the species breeds in the Madeiras, the Azores, the Salvage Islands, Cape Verde Islands and St Helena. Laying dates vary enormously with location. Out of the nesting season, the birds do not normally wander far from their breeding stations, but have been recorded off the United States and off Britain.

The easiest way of distinguishing the Madeiran from the Leach's petrel is that the white on the rump is an uninterrupted band across the bird.

LEACH'S STORM PETREL

(Syns: Leach's petrel, Leach's forked-tailed petrel)

Oceanodroma leucorhoa

Wing span 18 inches.

Two features help to identify this bird. The tail is deeply forked, and the white band across the rump is divided centrally by a black line extending from the centre of the tail feathers almost to touch the curve of the dark brown dorsal coverts. There is a greyish band on the top of the inner section of the wings, but this is not always very noticeable.

The bird does not habitually follow ships, but is, nevertheless, frequently seen from them. Its flight is diagnostic; bounding, almost butterfly-like, with frequent changes of direction.

Whereas the British storm petrel is the commoner in the eastern Atlantic, Leach's storm petrel is by far the more numerous off the coast of New England, where it breeds in large numbers. The species does, however, breed off northern Britain, in the Faroes and Iceland. The nest is usually in a shallow burrow excavated by the bird. The white egg is sometimes finely peppered with purple.

Eggs are laid in about May, the incubation and

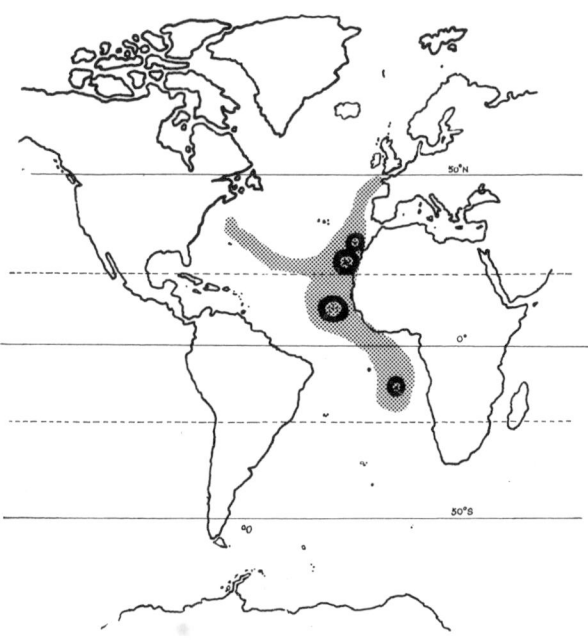
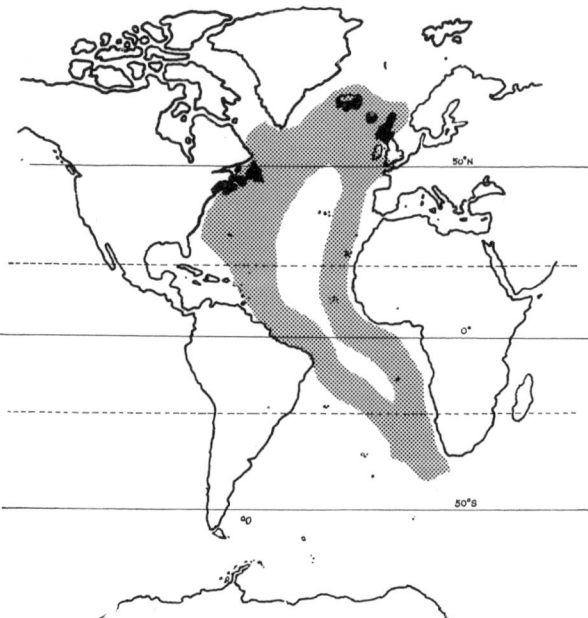

fledging periods total ninety-eight days. Out of the breeding season birds wander south as far as the Cape and northern South America. Like all the smaller members of the order it is nocturnal at the nesting site.

Channel and the Channel Islands.

The white egg, speckled with brown, is laid in December, usually among boulders or in rock crevices, though sometimes in burrows. The incubation and fledging periods total over ninety days.

WILSON'S STORM PETREL

Oceanites oceanicus

Wing span 15 inches.

It has been said that this bird is probably the most numerous of all sea birds. It is a native of the southern hemisphere, but migrates northward in the northern summer in vast numbers. The migratory circulations seem similar to that of the great and sooty shearwaters, but not only are Wilson's petrels recorded out at sea at this time of the year, they also come inshore in large numbers, sometimes crowding into such unlikely places as New York harbour.

The bird is slightly larger than the British storm petrel, but is similarly marked and has a square tail. Its distinguishing diagnostic feature is its very long legs – legs which protrude well beyond the tail when raised – and the feet, the webs of which are bright yellow. The wings are rounder and the flight is far steadier than those of other storm petrels. It is a ship follower.

The bird breeds on extreme south-western Atlantic islands and in Antarctica and ranges north in our summer as far as Newfoundland and the English

WHITE-FACED STORM PETREL

(Syns: frigate petrel, white-faced petrel)

Pelagodroma marina

Wing span 15 inches.

Though similar in shape and habit to the commoner storm petrels, this bird is quite different in coloration. With white cheeks, throat and belly, black cap, black wing tips and square black tail, the remainder of the back and wings pale grey streaked with a few dark bars, it is easily distinguished. There is a dark streak running backward from the eye. The black bill is very slim and straight and the tube nostrils practically non-existent. The legs are longer in relation to the size of the bird than those of any other storm petrel. They, too, are black, but the webs are bright orange.

White-faced storm petrels nest in small burrows on the Cape Verde and Canary Islands and also at Tristan da Cunha. In the North Atlantic, the egg, which is white, finely spotted with red, is laid in April and, in the South Atlantic, in October. Incubation takes forty-eight days. Like all young storm petrels,

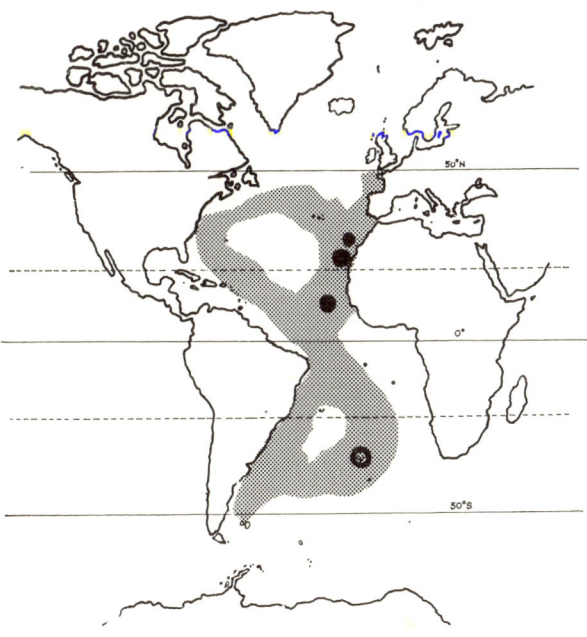

BIRDS OF THE ATLANTIC OCEAN

the chick is naked when newly hatched and fledging takes another fifty-eight days.

The species is not very numerous in the Atlantic, but in Australia breeds in enormous colonies. In the Atlantic, non-breeding birds wander to the coast of the Argentine, sometimes to North America and, very rarely, to Britain and northern Europe.

GREY-BACKED STORM PETREL
(Syns: night-bird, fire-bird)

Garrodia nereis

Wing span 16 inches.

A native of the Falkland Islands, Gough Island and South Georgia, this bird is similar to other storm petrels, but lacks the white rump. Instead, the back is dark grey, shading from nearly black on the head and wings to pale grey near the tail. The belly and underwing are white, the breast greyish-black. The bill and feet are black.

The egg is white with fine red dots, and is laid in November in hummocks of tussock grass, not in a burrow. Birds have been found nesting among colonies of rockhopper penguins. The adults and new generation of young leave the breeding grounds in April.

Distribution is very southerly and the bird is not recorded north of Capricorn.

The only other bird this could be confused with is

1. Wilson's Storm Petrel (enlarged study of bill).
2. Wilson's Storm Petrel.   3. British Storm Petrel.
4. Black-bellied Storm Petrel.   5. Grey-backed Storm Petrel.
6. Madeiran Storm Petrel.   7. White-faced Storm Petrel.

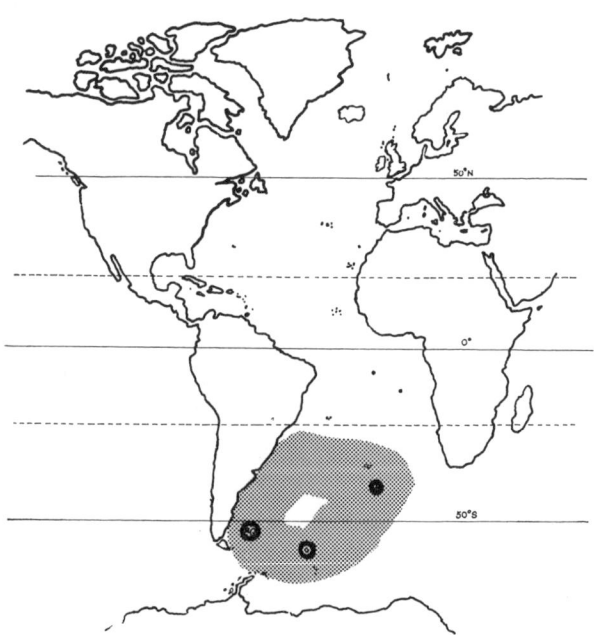

the white-faced storm petrel. The face and breast, however, are dark; it is a smaller bird and the webs are black, not orange.

BLACK-BELLIED STORM PETREL

Fregetta tropica

Wing span 17 inches.

The specific name of this bird would seem to be most misleading, for it is very unlikely, except during exceptional wanderings, that the bird ever enters the tropics. It is a pan-Antarctic species, breeding in South Georgia, the South Orkneys and South Shetlands, on Bouvet island and possibly in the Falkland Islands.

BIRDS OF THE ATLANTIC OCEAN

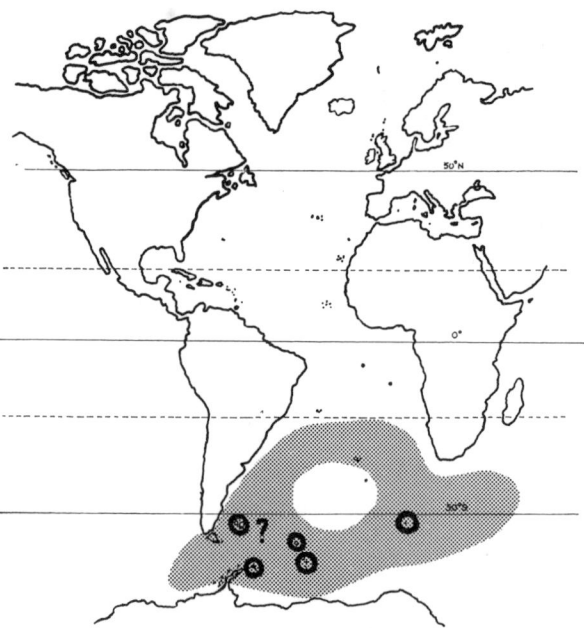

The bird is sooty black on its back – darkest on the head – the centre of the belly is black, slightly speckled with white and only the flanks and inner sections of the underwing are white. The white is sometimes very difficult to spot at sea.

Nesting time seems to vary, but in general the egg, which is white with a spattering of tiny pinkish-brown spots – sometimes in the form of a halo around the large end – is laid in early December. The nest itself is either in a burrow or in crevices among rocks, depending on the terrain.

Out of the breeding season the bird wanders over the oceans of the far south. It is by no means confined to the Atlantic sector of the southern oceans, being quite common in the region of New Zealand.

FAMILY *PELECANOIDIDAE* – DIVING PETRELS

Of the five species in this family, only three are Atlantic birds. Diving petrels are minute members of the order *TUBINARES* and, though more closely resembling the little auk of the northern hemisphere than any other, they are both scientifically and obviously tubenoses. The nostrils which protrude from the upper mandible have a peculiar flap-like valve across them.

They are, in other respects, auk-like birds with short whirring wings. Like auks, they have considerable difficulty in rising from the water in calm weather, and they dive, sometimes from the semi-airborne state, when alarmed by the approach of a vessel.

They are essentially birds of the south, being confined, except in one instance, between latitudes 35°S. and 60°S. The exception, the Peruvian diving petrel, is a bird of the Humbolt Current and is not, therefore, an Atlantic bird.

All diving petrels are so similar that they are not specifically distinguishable at sea. Locality is, however, a pretty safe guide.

COMMON DIVING PETREL
(Syn.: Falkland diver)

Pelecanoides urinatrix

Wing span 15 inches.

A bird of the Falkland Islands and the east coast of South America; it is small and auk-like; shiny black above and white beneath. There is a mottled collar across the upper breast. The bill is black and the legs, which are situated very far back, are deep cobalt blue. The feet are webbed. At the base of the lower mandible, there is a pouch similar to that of the whale-bird, which presumably has the same function – that of holding food-laden water, the water of which is expelled, leaving the food behind.

The single egg is white and is laid in July or August in a burrow. The birds assemble at sea in large numbers in the vicinity of the breeding ground as early as April. The principle breeding grounds are among the Falkland Island group, but the bird is also said to breed on Tristan da Cunha and Gough Island.

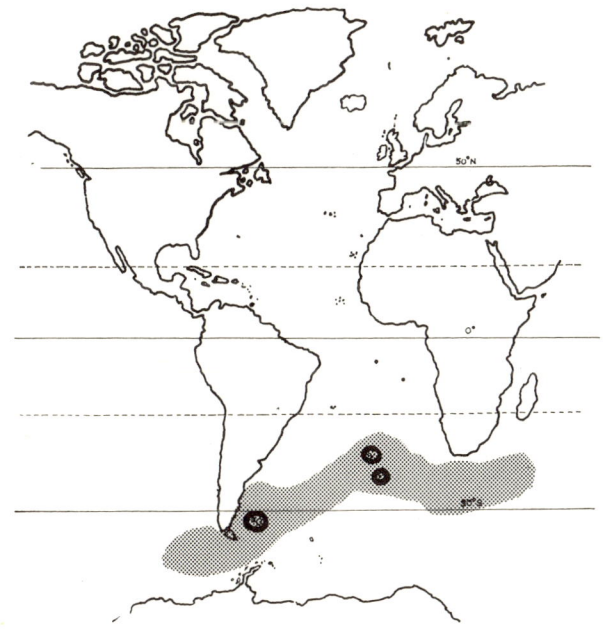

BIRDS OF THE ATLANTIC OCEAN

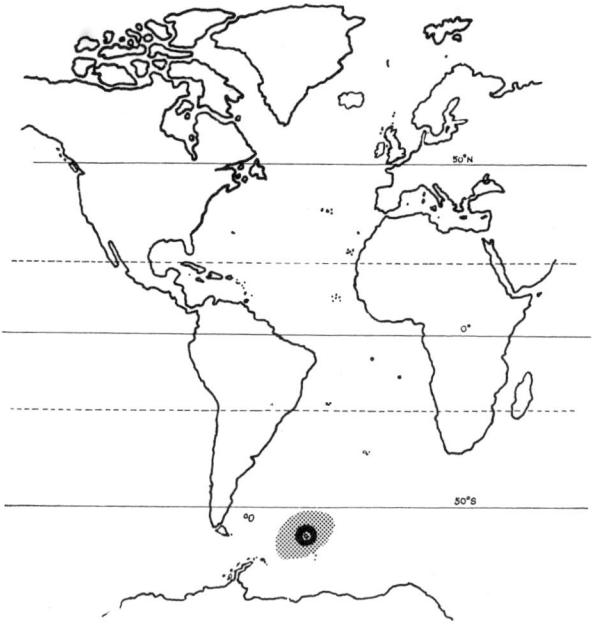
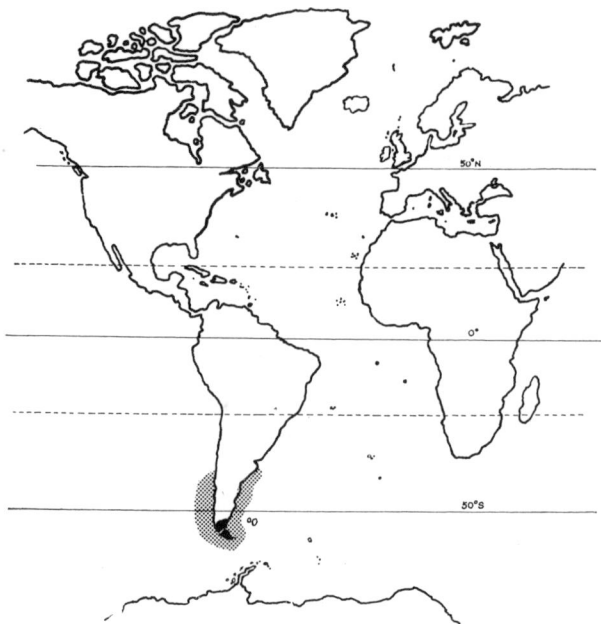

SOUTH GEORGIA DIVING PETREL

Pelecanoides georgicus

Wing span 14 inches.

This is the smallest of the three Atlantic members of the family, though the difference in size would definitely not be distinguishable at sea. The base of the lower mandible is wider than is that of the other two species and the pouch, when distended, more pronounced.

As the name implies, this species nests at South Georgia. The bird is essentially nocturnal when ashore. In no other way could this tiny species escape the ravages of predator gulls and skuas. The nests are in colonies and consist of burrows which are sometimes as much as six feet long, but which have been described as having entrances 'no bigger than a field-mouse's hole'.

Outside the breeding season, diving petrels seem to wander off over the ocean, which, in these latitudes, is almost always wild and stormy. It is amazing that so small and so clumsy a bird should survive these conditions.

The birds return from the sea to their burrows in November and their single white eggs are laid in December. The young find their way, fully fledged, to the sea at the end of March.

MAGELLAN DIVING PETREL

(Syns: Fuegian diving petrel, petrel sambullidor)

Pelecanoides magellani

Wing span 16 inches.

This, the largest of the three Atlantic diving petrels, differs from the others in having white tips to the feathers on its back. There is no collar on the breast. The bill is slightly slimmer than that of the other two species. None of these features, however, is clearly definable when the bird is on the wing.

The bird is a native of the coast and coastal islands of the southern tip of South America. Many are seen from ships passing through the Straits of Magellan.

Very little is known about the nesting localities or breeding habits of this species, although it is acknowledged that eggs are laid towards the end of November and that the young birds are fledged and ready to go to sea by March.

White-tailed Tropic Bird

ORDER *STEGANOPODES*

FAMILY *PHAËTHONTIDAE* – TROPIC BIRDS

Although these beautiful birds belong to the order *STEGANOPODES* – pelicans, cormorants, gannets and so on – the casual observer could well be forgiven for thinking that they were more closely related to terns. Their graceful, buoyant flight and the long, streamer tails are a joy to watch and seem far removed from the heavy, sometimes ponderous flight and comedy attitudes of some of their relations.

Only two species of tropic birds are natives of the Atlantic. There are, in fact, only three species in the world. Tropic birds, however, are well known to all who sail in tropical seas.

RED-BILLED TROPIC BIRD

(Syns: boatswain-bird, marlin spike)
Phaëthon aethereus

Wing span 43 inches.

This, the larger of the two Atlantic members of the family, is essentially a bird of the tropics. It is a large white bird with a heavy, sharp, coral-red or

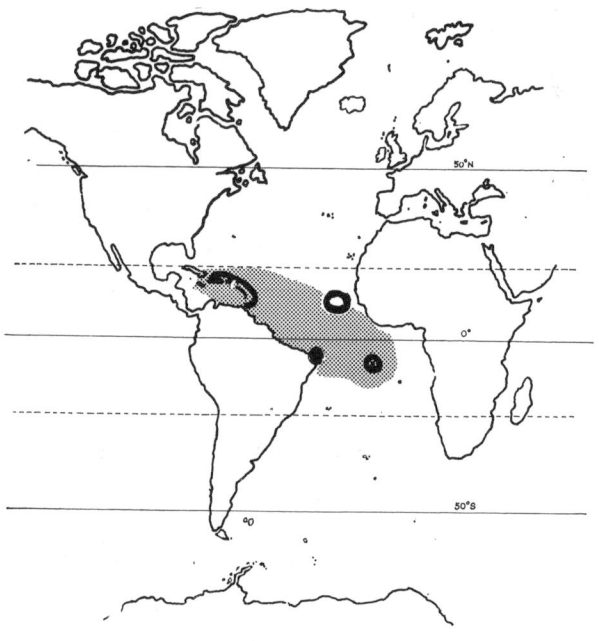

1. Red-billed Tropic Bird.   2. Red-billed Tropic Bird.
3. Common Diving Petrel.   4. Magellan Diving Petrel.
5. Common Diving Petrel.
6. Common Diving Petrel (gular sac extended).

BIRDS OF THE ATLANTIC OCEAN

orange bill. The central tail feathers are greatly elongated, giving the bird an accentuated, tern-like grace. There is a black band through each eye and a black bar on the wings. The back is finely barred with black. It is this barring which distinguishes the bird from its smaller near relation, the white-tailed tropic bird. The legs are pale yellow and the feet black.

The bird breeds on most of the tropical West Indies islands, the Cape Verde Islands, and Ascension Island. As with many tropical birds, egg laying is not seasonal, but takes place throughout the year. The single egg, which is laid in a crevice or on a high cliff ledge, is usually mottled purple or brown. The amount and colour of marking varies considerably.

The voice is hard, sharp and clear. In bright sunlight it is very often heard before the bird is spotted. It can best be described as a high pitched trill.

WHITE-TAILED TROPIC BIRD

(Syns: yellow-billed tropic bird, boatswain-bird, long-tail)

Phaëthon lepturus

Wing span 35 inches.

This bird has a more northerly limit to its range than the red-billed tropic bird. It nests in the Bahamas as well as the tropical islands of the Atlantic

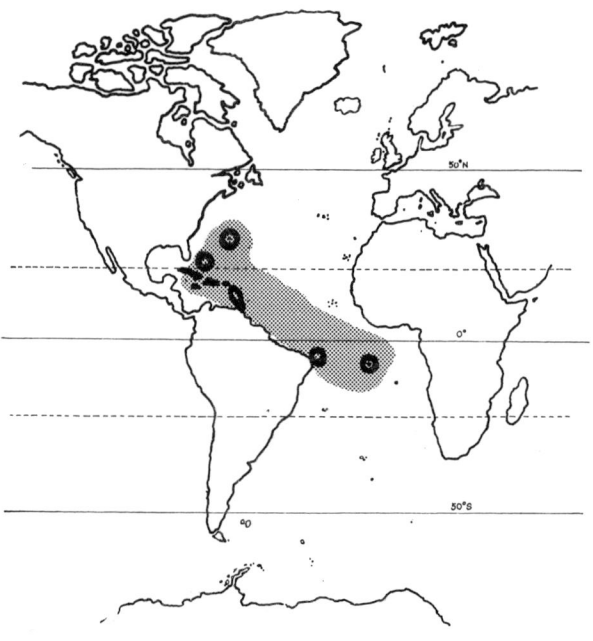

and as far north as Bermuda, where it is still abundant in the breeding season in spite of an immense increase in human population with all its attendant predatory fellow travellers.

It is similar, but smaller than the preceding species, the back, instead of being barred, is snow white except for the conspicuous black band over the wings. The bill varies in colour from yellow to red, even to black. There is sometimes a distinct rosy hue to the bird's white breast feathers.

Tropic birds fly with a steady, determined wing beat with short periods of glide. They have a very distinctive display flight in the vicinity of their nests, which could almost be compared to a horse shaking itself. The bird stops in flight and shivers from end to end and the shiver is greatly amplified by the time it reaches the end of the long tail. In courtship, two birds will fly one above the other and delicately touch the tips of each other's tail. There are few more lovely sights than the tropic bird flying overhead, its wings translucent beneath the high sun.

Normally, the single egg, heavily blotched with reddish-brown, is laid in any rock niche or ledge. Laying takes place in May, but as late as June in Bermuda. There the birds have mostly been driven from the inhabited islands and have resorted to the small islets which are still rat free. Unfortunately, the tropic birds are likely, on these islets, to be a threat to the survival of the few remaining cahows in the world.

In the small rock crevices to which Bermuda long-tails have now been driven, the long tail feathers sometimes have to be bent over in a hoop for the bird to fit into the nest cavity. The *'tick-er-tick-et'* of the tropic bird is a very familiar sound wherever the bird flies.

Outside the breeding season, they wander far off to sea and may be seen anywhere in tropical waters, thousands of miles from land.

FAMILY *PELECANIDAE* – PELICANS

Pelicans need no detailed description. Enormous and ungainly on land, they are nevertheless immensely strong fliers and dashing fishermen. They are not pelagic birds, in fact they hardly come within the vague but limiting definition of ocean birds, for they are birds of fresh water as well as the sea.

So large and conspicuous are they, however, and so entertaining and interesting to watch, that every sailor who visits the waters they frequent should know them and enjoy them. Only the species that are definitely seen at sea in some part of the Atlantic are included in this work.

PINK-BACKED PELICAN

Pelecanus rufescens

Wing span 91 inches.

This is an African pelican which frequents inland waters, but which may be seen at sea, particularly in the Cape region. It is a mainly white bird, tinged with pink in the breeding season. The primaries and some of the wing coverts are black so that the bird has a broad black border to the trailing edge of the wing. The tail is greyish-brown and so, in winter, are the wings. There is a marked crest on the back of the head and a tuft of long feathers forming a bib on the breast. The young are like adults in winter plumage.

They nest in colonies in trees, usually close to fresh water. The nests are of clumsy stick construction. Two or three chalky white eggs are laid.

AMERICAN WHITE PELICAN

Pelecanus erythrorhynchos

Wing span 108 inches.

This is much the largest of the Atlantic pelicans. It is a pure white bird with a very broad black band extending from the wing tips nearly to the body. There is a slight crest. The immature birds have a brown cap. The bill and feet are bright orange.

The pouch of this species is probably the most distendible of all pelicans. It will hold over four gallons of water. The birds hunt for food while waterborne. Large numbers of them assemble in a

BIRDS OF THE ATLANTIC OCEAN

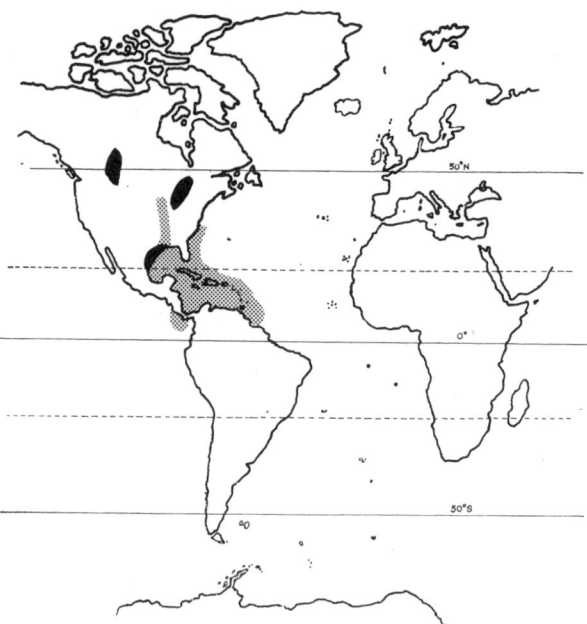

1. American White Pelican. 2. Brown Pelican.
3. Pink-backed Pelican.

line and drive fish towards the shore until they are cornered and then scoop them up in quantity.

They are powerful fliers, sometimes circling high and diving back to earth with a great commotion. When travelling any distance, they fly in Vee formation or in long lines. They flap and glide alternately, each bird's motions strictly synchronised with the rest of the flock.

They nest in large colonies on the isolated islands off the Texas coast; also on the Pacific coast of North America. Two chalky white eggs are laid in May or June, usually on bare ground or possibly on rotted vegetation.

White pelicans winter all round the Gulf coast and in the West Indies and Panama district.

BROWN PELICAN

Pelecanus occidentalis

Wing span 80 inches.

This is the most spectacular fisherman of all birds. A flock of brown pelicans, diving from a height of perhaps thirty feet headlong into the sea, at a distance looks like some naval action of bygone days, so high are the plumes of water showered into the air. The birds do not, however, dive very deep. They feed essentially on surface shoals and re-appear on the surface almost as soon as the immense splash they create has subsided.

Although appearing rather drab brown when seen afar, the brown pelican is actually a bird of many colours and several different garbs. In breeding plumage, the adult bird is grey with rich chocolate head and neck, down each side of which runs a broad cream stripe. After the post-nuptial moult, there is a change to chocolate face and solid white neck. The immature bird is grey or brown-grey all over except for a white belly. All birds have a marked crest.

Brown pelicans are rather timid and foolish birds. If alarmed by an aircraft or fast motor-boat, they panic. But instead of taking off – a long and laborious business for a fish-laden bird of such proportions – they frequently just put their heads under water, shut their eyes and, presumably, hope for the best.

They are the most truly marine of all pelicans, fishing at sea and always nesting by salt water. They nest in colonies, usually in low trees, though sometimes on the ground. The eggs – three rather dirty white ones – are laid throughout the year. The

BIRDS OF THE ATLANTIC OCEAN

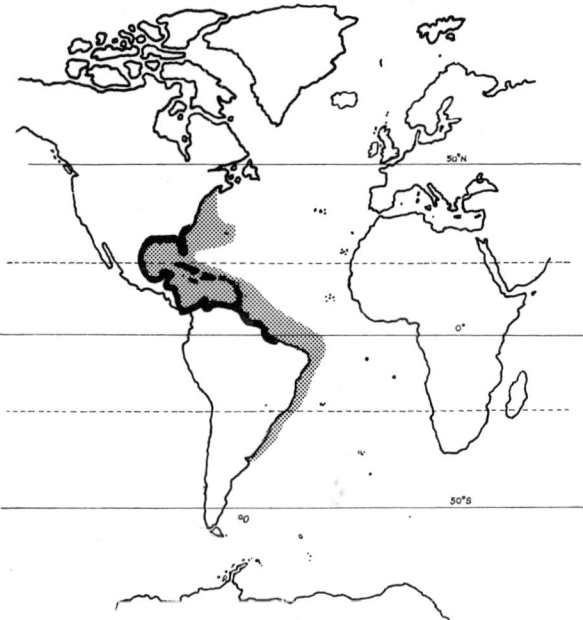

breeding season of individual pairs recurs at less than annual intervals. Colonies can be found on small islands throughout the West Indies and off the tropical coasts of America, from South Carolina to the mouth of the Amazon.

Non-breeding birds wander as far north as New England and as far south as the Argentine. The species has even been recorded as far out in the ocean as Bermuda.

FAMILY *SULIDAE* – GANNETS AND BOOBIES

Gannets are large, cigar-shaped birds with long, pointed wings, large heads and very big, sharp bills. They have large eyes which, by virtue of their juxtaposition with the bill, look very accentuated and fierce.

It is perhaps surprising that they are included in the order of pelicans, but there are great similarities, though these may not, at first, be apparent; the relatively large head, the pointed bill, the short, web-footed legs, and the gannet's pouch which has nearly disappeared.

Gannets fish by diving from a height. Moreover, they swim quite a distance under water in pursuit of their prey. Unlike pelicans, gannets and boobies are essentially sea birds.

NORTHERN GANNET

(Syns: gannet, solan goose)

Morus bassanus

Wing span 74 inches.

The adult gannet is a sparkling white bird with a yellowish head and jet-black wing tips. The wings are long and pointed, and so is the tail. The bluish horn-coloured beak is sharp, enormous and vicious-looking, with the gape extending well back. There is a vertical line through the piercing eyes, which are picked out by black bordering. The young birds – and they do not attain adult plumage for four years – are mottled brown, black and white.

Gannets nest in densely packed colonies on the flat tops of rocky islets or stacks. There are five such colonies on the western side of the North Atlantic and seventeen on the European side. The birds are quarrelsome and noisy in the colony. The nest is usually a mound of seaweed on dropping-drenched ground. One egg is usually laid in May and the chicks are naked and helpless when hatched. At twelve or thirteen weeks old, the young are deserted for ten days before they tumble and flap to the sea below.

A gannetry is a marvellous sight and sound; thousands of birds wheeling round and round – usually the same way as at a well-ordered airport – noisy and animated social activity on the ground, and the continual hubbub of many thousands of gutteral, cackling voices.

Out of the breeding season, gannets wander south, singly or in small groups, to the Gulf of Mexico in the west and to Madeira, the Canary Islands and North Africa in the east.

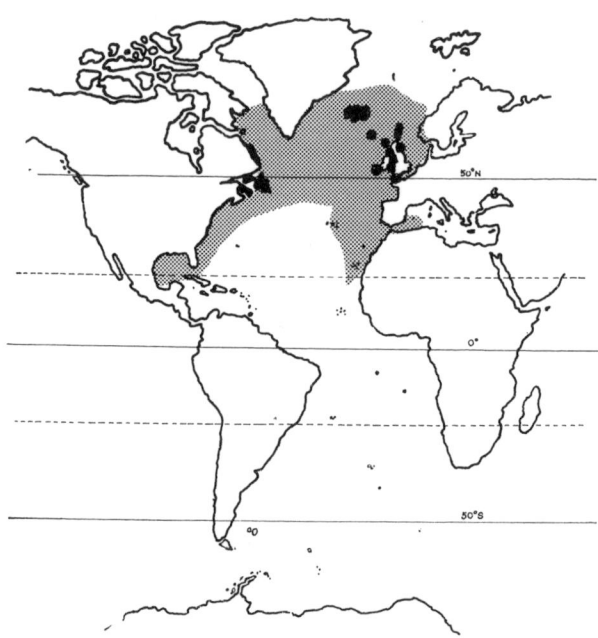

ORDER *STEGANOPODES*

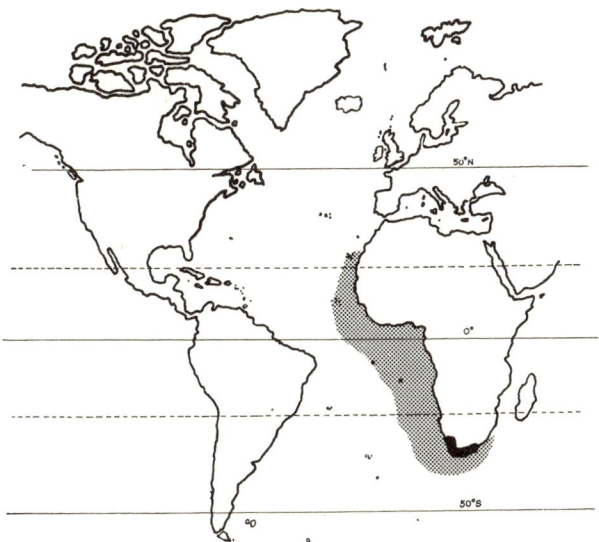
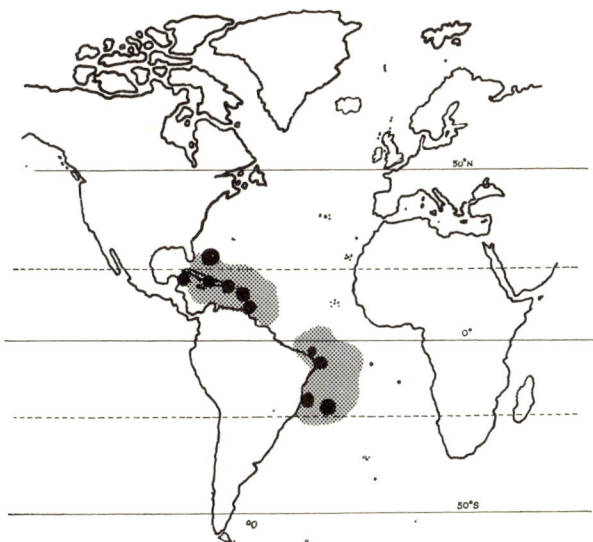

CAPE GANNET

(Syn.: malagash)

Morus capensis

Wing span 72 inches.

This bird is very similar to the northern gannet and is probably a race of the super species *Bassanus*. Where the northern gannet is black, however, the Cape gannet is a brownish-black. The bill is blue and the feet are black.

Off the south African coast where the bird breeds, a regular industry exists in the collection of guano. The egg is laid in September and the domestic arrangements are similar to those of the northern gannet.

Out of the breeding season, birds wander as far north as Dakar and may even reach the Canaries, where it is quite possible their range overlaps that of the northern gannet.

BLUE-FACED BOOBY

Sula dactylatra

Wing span 64 inches.

These birds are similar in general shape to gannets; in fact they are the gannets of warmer waters – a rose by any other name . . . ! The species is distinguished as follows. The whole of the trailing edges of the wings are dark brownish-black. The edge of the pointed tail is brownish-black. The bills of the females are pink at the base; those of the males orange. The area around the base of the bill – the face – is very dark blue, almost black.

Immature birds are a smoky-brown flecked with white above, but they have white underparts. There is a pale patch where the neck ends and the back begins, and again where the back ends and the tail begins.

Boobies do not fly away when approached by man. They stand and defiantly hold their ground. Thus they are easily caught and this habit may be the origin of the name. Blue-faced boobies feed mostly on flying fish. They will dive and follow fish for some distance under water. As they follow shoals of flying fish, they are frequently seen well out of sight of land in tropical waters.

They nest in loose colonies on the ground on islands from the Bahamas in the north, all round the Caribbean; also on Ascension Island.

There is no set breeding season. Eggs are laid throughout the year. There are usually two, but, as they hatch at widely separated intervals, the older chick dominates the younger which consequently seldom survives.

RED-FOOTED BOOBY

Sula sula

Wing span 60 inches.

This is a very much smaller bird than the preceding species. The colouring is similar; a white bird with a

BIRDS OF THE ATLANTIC OCEAN

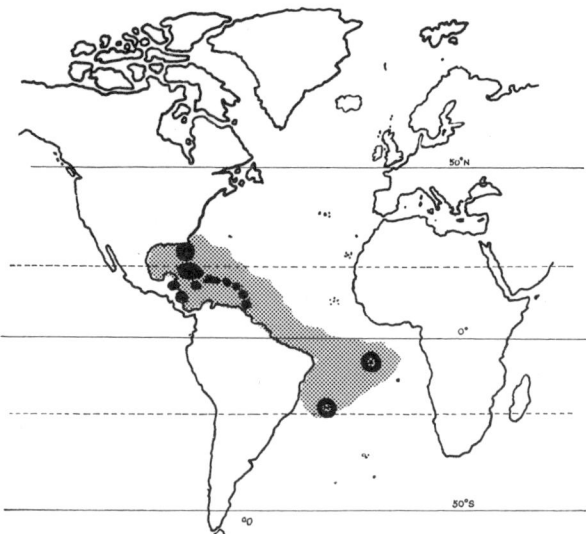

1. Cape Gannet. 2. Brown Booby. 3. Blue-faced Booby.
4. Red-footed Booby.

broad, dark brown trailing edge to its wings, but with a very elongated tail which is usually all white. The feet, from which of course it gets its name, are bright red. There are, however, many variations in coloration which are not truly understood. Maybe they are just individual recognition markings.

The red-footed booby is a tree nester. The nest is made of sticks, sometimes in a mere bush, sometimes in quite a tall tree. The single pale blue egg may be laid at any time of the year. There are colonies on islands which have suitable vegetation in the West Indies, on the Florida coast and at Ascension and South Trinidad.

Red-footed boobies range the tropical seas in search of flying fish and squids, sometimes flying low over the wave tops and sometimes at heights of twenty to thirty feet from which they dive on their prey.

on the ground in the Bahamas, the West Indies and islands off Central America.

Two pale blue eggs are usually laid at any time of the year, but only one chick survives. When not intent on breeding matters they wander considerable distances and have been recorded as far north as Massachusetts.

BROWN BOOBY

Sula leucogastra

Wing span 56 inches.

The brown booby is the commonest member of its family in the tropical west Atlantic. It is small and very dark brown with a white belly and yellow legs. The immature bird is dark all over. Both adult and immature have a much darker and less speckled plumage than the immature gannet.

Brown boobies hunt in flocks and dive frequently for their food – flying fish, half-beaks and mullet. They can frequently be seen ranging low over the water in the Caribbean. They rest on trees, but nest

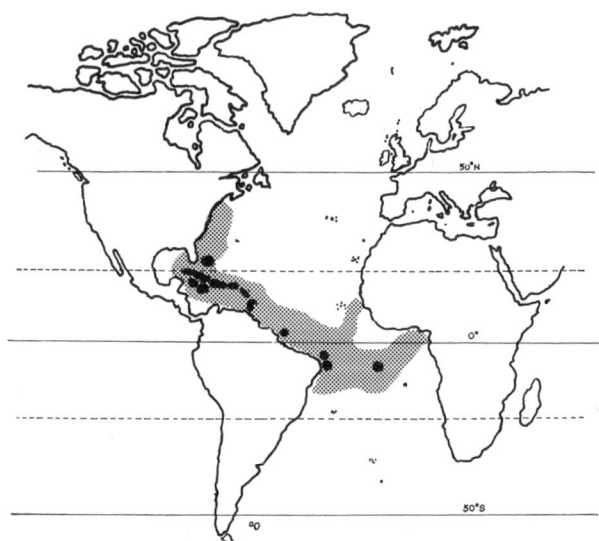

FAMILY *PHALACROCORACIDAE* – CORMORANTS

The sea birds of this family are long-necked, large-winged birds with slender, hooked bills. They are long shaped and somewhat grotesque in appearance, but, in fact, possess beautifully streamlined bodies, admirably adapted for swimming under water. Their legs are short and all four toes are joined by webs. They have relatively long wedge-shaped tails. The name cormorant means 'sea crow'. There is, however, no resemblance between a cormorant and a crow, except that they are both mainly black.

Cormorants, of course, are fish eaters. They dive to chase fish under water, usually by springing from a surface swimming position in a neat loop to plunge head-first beneath the sea.

A curious adaptation possessed by the family is that a cormorant can swim on the surface in almost any condition of buoyancy, from being right on the surface like a cork to semi-submerged with only the head showing.

This is not, as may be thought, a defiance of the laws of Archimedes, but judicious use of many air sacs which can, like a submarine's ballast tanks, be flooded or not, at will.

DOUBLE-CRESTED CORMORANT

Phalacrocorax auritus

Wing span 51 inches.

The name, double-crested, stems from the fact that this large cormorant has two tufts of white feathers, one on each side of the crown, during the breeding season. It is the most widespread of North American cormorants, ranging from New England in the north, right down through Central America and the Caribbean to the Equator.

The adult bird is black, shot with green and brown. There is an orange patch at the base of the yellowish bill. The young are greyish-brown with paler underparts.

Double-crested cormorants breed all down the North American seaboard and on the Bahamas. The nest is a bulky structure of sticks, seaweed and grass. Sometimes it is placed in a tree, sometimes on

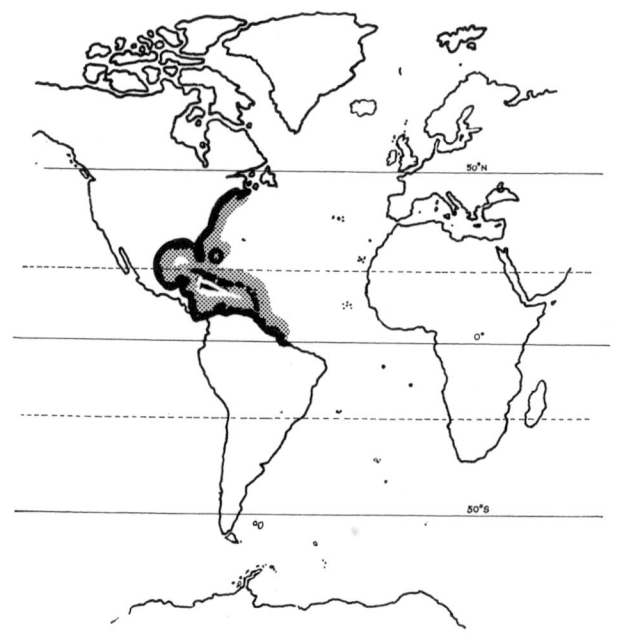

ORDER *STEGANOPODES*

the ground on a rocky islet. Three or four pale blue, elongated eggs are laid any time from March to June, depending on latitude. The young, when first hatched, are black and naked.

OLIVACEOUS CORMORANT

(Syns: American cormorant, Mexican cormorant, bigua cormorant)

Phalacrocorax olivaceus

Wing span 40 inches.

For a cormorant, this is a small, slim bird. It is black with a green sheen and, in the breeding season, has a distinctive white line between the feathered neck and the naked throat pouch. The pouch is bright orange.

The range of the olivaceous cormorant is very considerable as it seems just as happy in the tropics as in the wind-swept far south of the American continent. It may be seen anywhere from the Bahamas, south to Cape Horn; never, however, very far from the coast. Large numbers congregate in the lakes of the Panama Canal.

These cormorants nest in colonies in trees, on rocks or on the ground. Nesting material varies from just a few sprays of seaweed to considerable quantities of sticks. The nest may be a mere mound or it may be a large platform. The four pale bluish eggs are laid through the year, depending on locality.

COMMON CORMORANT

(Syn.: European cormorant)

Phalacrocorax carbo

Wing span 58 inches.

This is the largest of all the cormorants and probably the best known to Europeans. It is a large, ungainly bird with, when in breeding plumage, a large white patch at the throat and white patches on each thigh. The cormorant is a very familiar bird in coastal districts and in the vicinity of harbours throughout its range, which is almost world wide. On buoys and navigation marks in piloted waters, cormorants stand about, hanging themselves out to dry, so to speak. With feet slightly splayed, neck stretched and wings held out like a cloakroom attendant holding two very wet mackintoshes, the cormorant adds comical, ungainly decoration to the object on which it stands.

Cormorants are all good divers and common cormorants will tackle quite large fish. It is said that they cannot swallow their catch till they reach the surface and it is for this reason that the Chinese have trained them to catch fish commercially for them. If a cormorant catches a large eel, it will come to the surface many times with the eel wrapped wriggling around its neck and body. While the eel still struggles, and if the cormorant cannot yet swallow its catch, the bird will dive again and again, presumably to drown it. This relentless struggle can go on

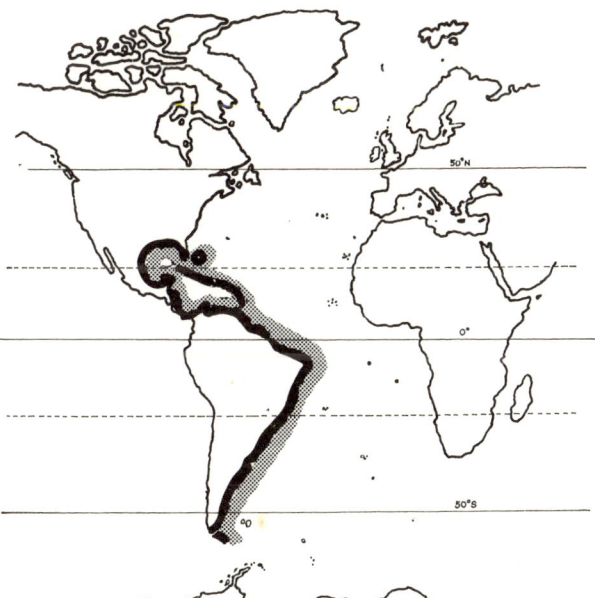
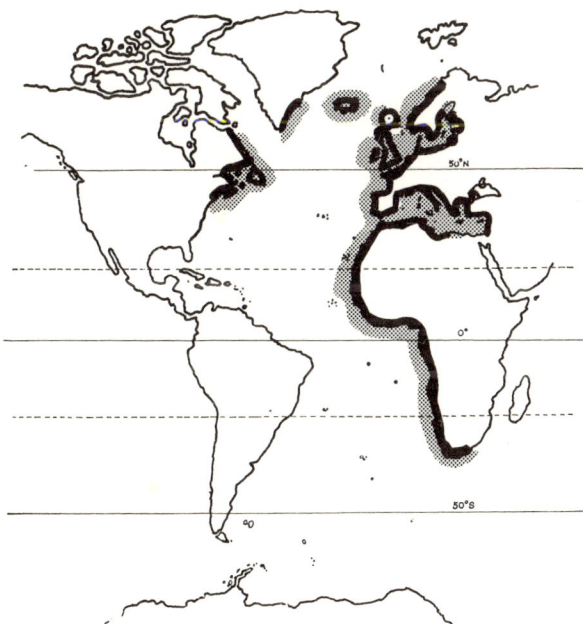

for up to half an hour before the bird finally swims off, victoriously swallowing its long meal bit by bit, the grotesque movements of its neck showing clearly that though the eel may have conceded victory it is still capable of a last convulsive twist.

On the eastern seaboard of the Atlantic, common cormorants nest on most coasts right down to Cape Province. On the American side they do not spread south beyond Maine. The three or four pale blue, chalky-surfaced eggs are laid in April in northern temperate zones, at any time in the tropics and in August in southern temperate zones. The nest is a mound of seaweed, grass, sticks or any other flotsam, usually placed on a cliff ledge or on the top of a rocky islet.

Immature common cormorants are a dirty greyish-brown with pale, sometimes almost white bellies.

A race, *P.c.sinensis,* which in breeding plumage has a profusion of white plumes on its head, giving the impression of an almost white head, occurs in Europe. It breeds in Denmark, Belgium, Holland and France. Out of the breeding season it is indistinguishable from any other common cormorant.

CAPE CORMORANT
Phalacrocorax capensis

Wing span 42 inches.

This is a small, entirely dark cormorant. It is jet black except for the foreneck and breast which is very dark brown. The naked skin of the face and throat is yellow.

It is a native of south Africa where it plays an important commercial role as a producer of guano. Enormous flocks occur all round the African coast from the Congo to Durban.

The three or four long, chalky white eggs are laid throughout the year in a nest which is built of varying amounts of weed and flotsam on small, rocky islets off the coast. The young Cape cormorant is a brownish bird with the neck and chest almost white.

BANK CORMORANT
Phalacrocorax neglectus

Wing span 48 inches.

Not only is this south African cormorant much larger than the Cape cormorant, but it frequently has white plumes scattered about the neck and sometimes a conspicuous white patch on its rump.

The bank cormorant has a very limited range and is found only on the Atlantic seaboard of the Republic of South Africa, where it nests on islands off the coast. Eggs are laid in August or September; early in the southern spring.

The name, bank cormorant, is derived from the fact that it spends most of its life among the seaweed beds of the fishing banks. It is described as having a 'loud melancholy cry'. Young birds are a brownish-black.

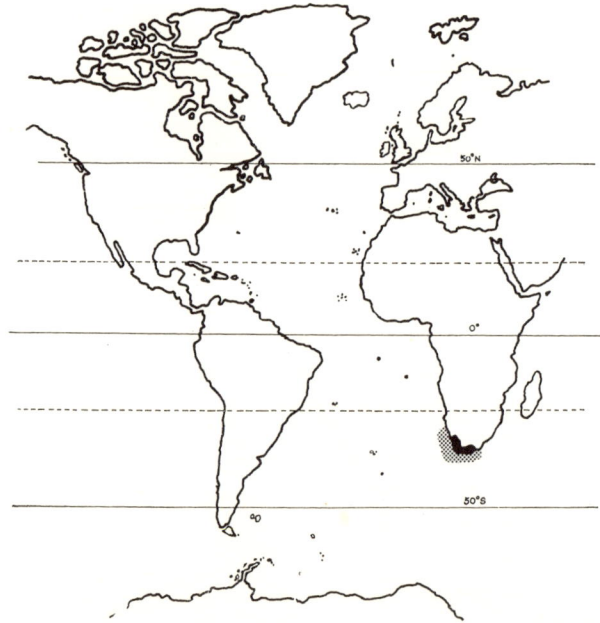

SHAG

(Syn.: green cormorant)

Phalacrocorax aristotelis

Wing span 44 inches.

The shag is distinguished from the common cormorant – the only member of the family whose range overlaps its own – by its smaller size and slimmer build, its all dark plumage which is generously shot with green, and its marked crest which, on occasions, is erectable.

These are birds of rugged coasts. The west coast of Scotland, western Ireland and the Devon and Cornwall peninsula abound with them. Where their range overlaps that of their larger cousin, *carbo*, they inhabit the lower, wetter ledges of their chosen nesting sites. Their food is nearly exclusively small eels, whereas although the cormorant can and does tackle large eels, its staple diet is flat-fish.

The cormorant family swim underwater using their feet only, unlike many other diving birds who swim with their wings.

The nest of the shag is usually a mound of seaweed which, when not washed away by storm, grows bigger year by year. The birds nest in small, open colonies. The long, pale blue, chalky-surfaced eggs are laid in March or April.

Where conditions suit, the shag is widely distributed, breeding from Iceland all around the Atlantic coast of Europe, and in the Mediterranean from the Balearics to the Aegean. They are also to be found on some sections of the Moroccan Atlantic coast.

Young birds are brown above and whitish beneath. They have no crest.

ROCK SHAG

(Syn.: Magellan cormorant)

Phalacrocorax magellanicus

Wing span 40 inches.

This is a small black and white cormorant of the extreme southern coast of South America. In full breeding plumage, the bird is black on its back, head, neck and upper breast and white on its belly. It has rather a long, pointed tail. There is a flash of white on the cheek, which consists of a clump of long, narrow, white plumes. In winter, the throat and underside of the neck are white and the cheek plumes are absent. Unlike most cormorants, the throat feathers extend forward to the lower mandible of the beak. The face, however, is still bare, the skin on this bare patch being bright red. The bill itself is black, but the feet are flesh-coloured with black webs.

The rock shag is found on the coast of Tierra del Fuego and up the south-east coast of South America as far as latitude 44°S., also in the Falkland Islands.

It is a rock breeder, laying its eggs in November at the northern end of its range and as late as January in the south. The young are black.

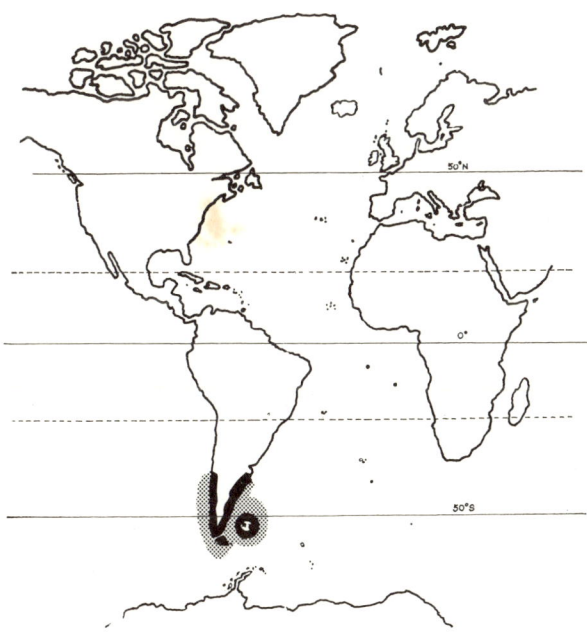

BIRDS OF THE ATLANTIC OCEAN

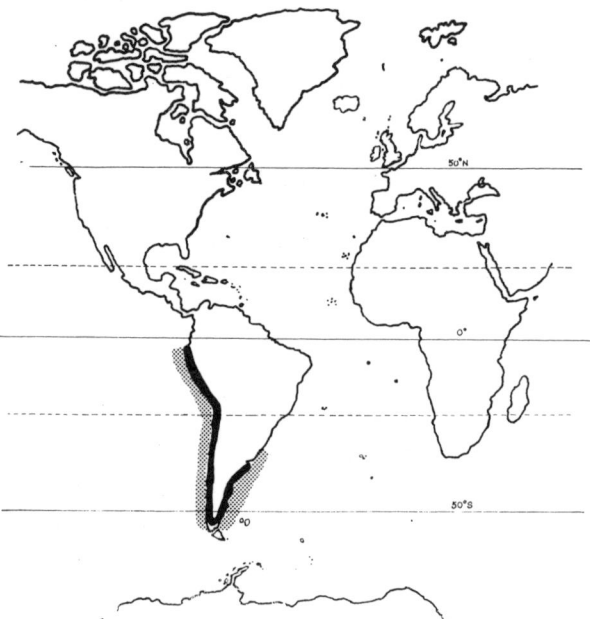

RED-FOOTED SHAG

(Syn.: red-legged cormorant)

Phalacrocorax gaimardi

Wing span 40 inches.

This very handsome little cormorant has approximately the same range as the previous species. It is, however, very easily recognised as it is a grey bird with bright red face and legs. In the breeding season, there are white spots on the face, otherwise the plumage is all grey, darker on the top and paler beneath.

It is mainly a Pacific bird, but may be seen on the Patagonian coast where it is a solitary nester. It lays its eggs very late for a southern hemisphere bird; in May. None have been reported from the Falkland Islands.

Young birds are dark brown with a few white spots; rather mottled beneath.

BLUE-EYED SHAG

(Syns: king shag, blue-eyed cormorant)

Phalacrocorax atriceps

Wing span 49 inches.

The blue-eyed shag, whose range overlaps that of the rock shag quite considerably, is distinguished

1. Common Cormorant (immature).   2. Shag (immature).
3. Shag.   4. Common Cormorant.
5. Common Cormorant (southern type).
6. Double-crested Cormorant.
7. Double-crested Cormorant (immature).
8. Olivacious Cormorant.   9. Cape Cormorant.
10. Bank Cormorant.   11. Rock Shag.   12. Blue-eyed Shag.
13. Reed Cormorant.   14. Reed Cormorant.   15. Rock Shag.

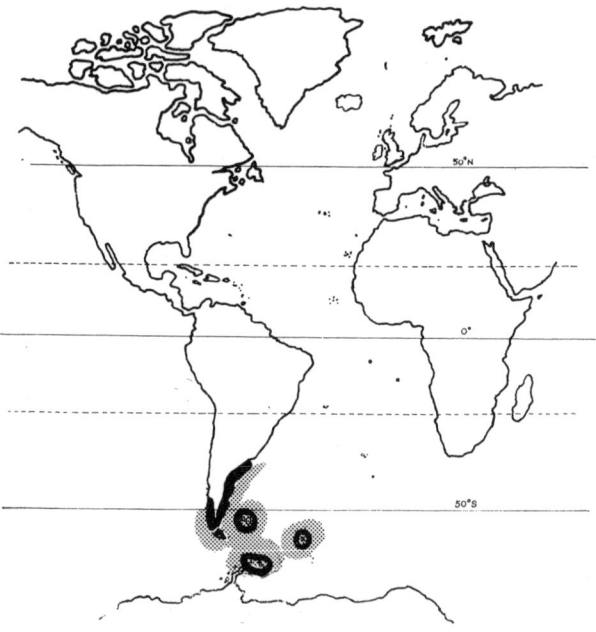

BIRDS OF THE ATLANTIC OCEAN

from that species by its larger size. Also distinguishing is its white throat and neck even in the breeding season, the throat feathers that do not come forward to the lower mandible, the throat that is naked like other cormorants and is blue, not red – and the white bar on the wings.

This bird is very widespread around the southern end of South America and breeds on most sub-Antarctic islands. Races of the super species vary from island group to island group, which is not surprising as cormorants do not normally cover large distances over the ocean. They are ground or rock nesters and lay their eggs in November.

REED CORMORANT

Phalacrocorax africanus

Wing span 34 inches.

The reed cormorant hardly qualifies as an ocean bird as it breeds mostly on the lakes and rivers of Africa. It is, however, frequently seen at sea and does, in fact, breed on islands in the vicinity of the Cape of Good Hope.

It is a very small cormorant and has a short neck and long tail. The plumage is mainly black. The throat is dull white and, in the breeding season, there are a few white plumes protruding from the face and neck. The naked skin of the face and throat is yellow and the feet are black.

The young are brown on top and a dirty, yellowish-white beneath.

The birds which breed on the Cape coast lay their eggs in September.

FAMILY *FREGATIDAE* – FRIGATE BIRDS

Frigate birds, or man-o'-war birds or hawks, as they are sometimes called, are probably the easiest of all sea birds to recognise. They have slim bodies, long, forked tails and enormous, broad, pointed wings. They are black above with varying amounts of white beneath. Young birds have white heads, a colour they keep for at least two years when the dark plumage is attained.

Frigates are the most aerial of all sea birds and never land on level ground or on water. They are airborne nearly as much as swifts. They feed by attacking gulls, terns, boobies and pelicans and, by the threat of injury from their long, hook-ended bills, make their victims disgorge their food; a method of hunting, in fact, very akin to that of skuas. Frigate birds also feed on fish, molluscs and jellyfish, for which they dive to pluck from the surface of the sea.

Though almost continuously airborne, they are not in any way pelagic birds and are seldom seen far from the tropical islands they frequent. Most of the day is spent sailing high over the water, occasionally diving for food while, at night, they usually perch on trees or other elevated features from which they can easily take off at dawn.

ASCENSION FRIGATE BIRD

Fregata aquila

Wing span 79 inches.

This is the only frigate bird with entirely black or brown plumage in both sexes. The feathers of the back are shot with green. The male bird has a red, distendible pouch at the base of its bill. The female is bigger than the male and the upper breast is brown. The feet of the adult male are red; the legs – like those of all the family – being short. All four toes are joined by a web. The immature birds have white heads and dark brown plumage.

They breed in large colonies on Boatswain-bird Island, near Ascension Island, building large nests of sticks in trees or on rocks. The single, white egg is laid in February. The chicks are hatched naked, but soon acquire a covering of white down. The birds are jealous nesters, guarding their houses and their

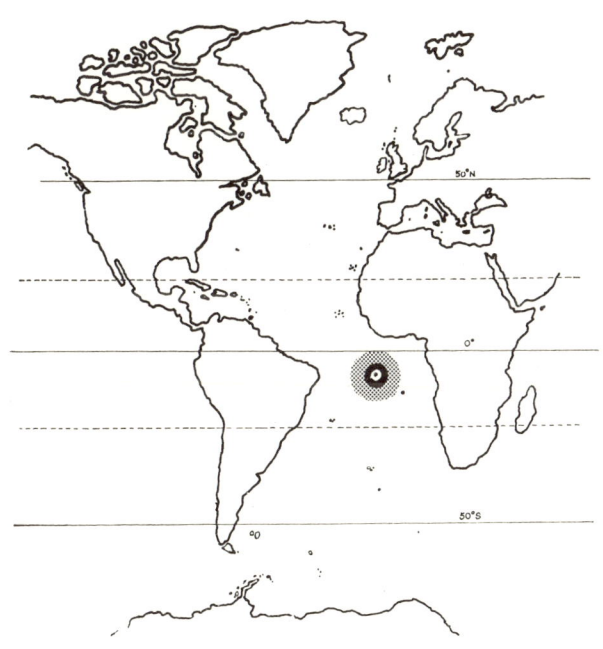

young continually. This is just as well as unattended nests are liable to be robbed by other birds in the colony. A nesting frigate bird has no scruples about robbing sticks, eggs or young from other nests.

Ascension frigate birds do not wander more than a hundred miles from their breeding grounds.

MAGNIFICENT FRIGATE BIRD

(Syn.: man-o'-war bird)

Fregata magnificens

Wing span 90 inches.

This wonderful bird is widely spread throughout the tropical Atlantic. For the first two years of their life, the sexes are alike, having white heads and underparts, and bronze-shot back feathers and tail. In adult plumage, the larger female has a greenish-black head, a white breast and otherwise bronze-black feathers. The male is all dark with an orange throat pouch. In the breeding season, when the pouch is frequently blown up in display, it becomes a vivid crimson.

The species nests in colonies on the Bahamas, the West Indies, in Mexico and around the coast of the Caribbean to tropical northern South America; also on the Cape Verde Islands. They sometimes wander as far north as Bermuda.

The large, stick nests are placed sometimes in trees, but more often on rocks or any suitable mounds which satisfy the demands of long winged take-off. The single, white egg is laid in February.

GREAT FRIGATE BIRD

Fregata minor

Wing span 85 inches.

Though the English name of this species is possibly misleading, the specific name gives the correct clue for it is smaller than the magnificent frigate bird. The female, however, of the great frigate bird is about the same size, if not bigger, than the male *magnificens*. The two species are very similar in appearance, but their ranges, which hardly overlap, are diagnostic.

The plumage of the male is mainly black, shot with green, the bill is black or blue, the distensible pouch is red and the feet anything from black to pink. There is a brown band across the wings. The female has a greyish-white foreneck and throat, and a white breast. The young have white heads and underparts.

The birds range along the Brazilian coast and the South Atlantic ocean. They nest in colonies in trees at South Trinidad Island, off the coast of Brazil, often in the colonies of other species that they harass and prey upon.

The single, oval, chalky-white egg is laid in March.

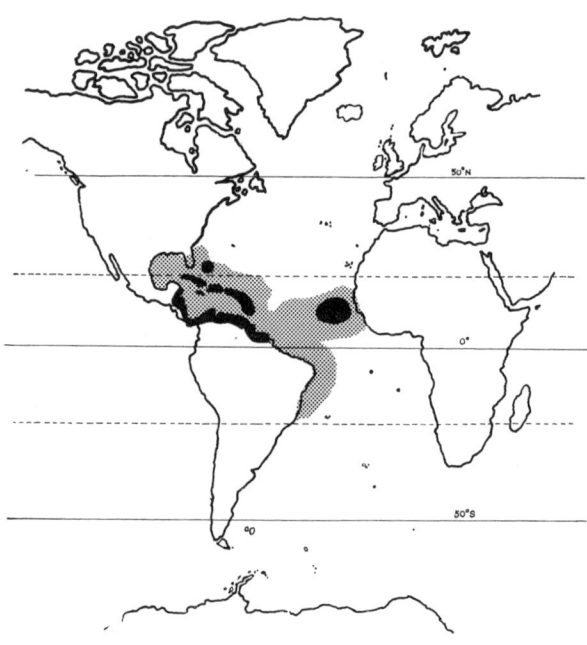
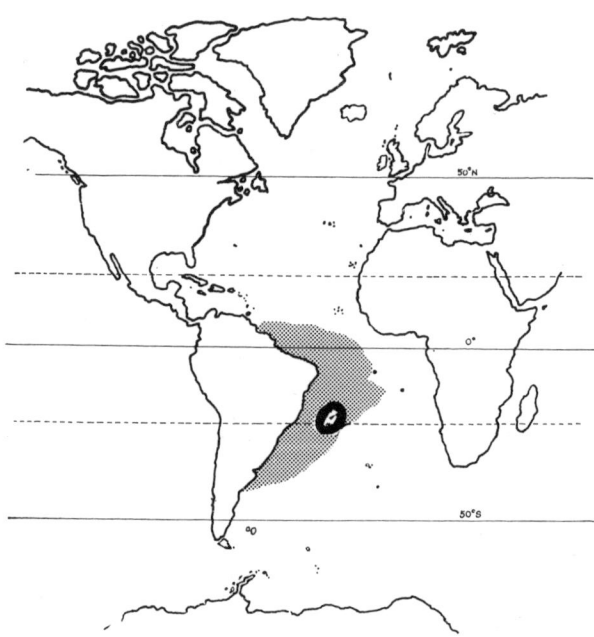

Magnificent Frigate Bird

BIRDS OF THE ATLANTIC OCEAN

LESSER FRIGATE BIRD

Fregata ariel

Wing span 72 inches.

This smaller, South Atlantic frigate bird is easily distinguished from others of its family. Both sexes have a conspicuous white patch on their sides, under the wings. It is, in fact, a world-wide species, being commonest in oceans other than the Atlantic. In the Atlantic, where it is almost rare, it nests at South Trinidad, where its single, white egg is laid in April.

Like others of its family, it has a long, narrow, forked tail. This tail appears normally long, straight and narrow as the bird sails effortlessly round in the tropical sun. It is only occasionally that the fork is opened to reveal its full extent.

Do not be deceived by the leisurely, effortless, almost lazy flight of the frigate bird. It can easily catch up with pelicans, cormorants, boobies or gulls to force them to disgorge its next meal.

1. **Magnificent Frigate Bird (adult male with gular sac extended).**
2. **Magnificent Frigate Bird (immature).** 3. **Great Frigate Bird.**
4. **Ascension Frigate Bird.** 5. **Lesser Frigate Bird.**
6. **Magnificent Frigate Bird (adult male).**

ORDER *LARO-LIMICOLAE*

FAMILY *PHALAROPODIDAE* – PHALAROPES

Phalaropes are waders and would not be expected, therefore, to come under the heading of ocean birds. But, in fact, out of the breeding season they may be seen in any part of the ocean, sometimes in quite large flocks. Other waders may cross the oceans of the world on migration, but no other settles on the water or lives at sea for a large part of its life.

Because of its exceptional way of life, the phalaropes have two important adaptations. Their feet are partly webbed, each toe, like those of the coot, having an individual lobed web of its own. Their plumage is like that of a duck or a goose, consisting of ordinary feathers on the top, with a secondary insulating coat of down underneath.

The three species of phalarope nest in the far north and are circum-polar. In winter, they wander south across the oceans of the world. When met at sea, they appear to be completely fearless, allowing man to approach very close without showing any signs of alarm. They swim in a very upright, buoyant fashion – a habit which makes recognition easy at some distance.

The females of the family are larger than the males and they are the ones which come out in gay colours in the breeding season. In fact, the female does the courting and leaves the incubation and brood raising to the male. She only lays the eggs. What you might call a Leap Year bird!

GREY PHALAROPE
(Syn.: red phalarope)
Phalaropus fulicarius

Wing span 15 inches.

This species is a gaudy chestnut colour in breeding plumage, with a striated back, white cheeks and grey primaries with a white bar on them. The female is larger and brighter than the male. In winter, the bird is nearly white with a grey back and black eye-stripe. The bill is slender, slightly down-curved and yellow.

When seen at sea, the bird will always be in its winter plumage, which is very similar to that of the red-necked phalarope. The bill, however, is stouter and yellow, not black. The back is a more uniform grey which may have led to its name.

The breeding grounds of the grey phalarope are circum-polar, in Alaska, Arctic Canada, Greenland, Iceland, Spitzbergen, Novaya Zemlya and northern Siberia. The nest is a mere hollow in the ground with a few wisps of grass as lining. Three to four eggs are laid in June. They are pointed, greeny-buff or cream and boldly blotched with brown. The young are born fluffy and can run as soon as hatched. The nest is always near water of some sort, usually fresh.

ORDER *LARO-LIMICOLAE*

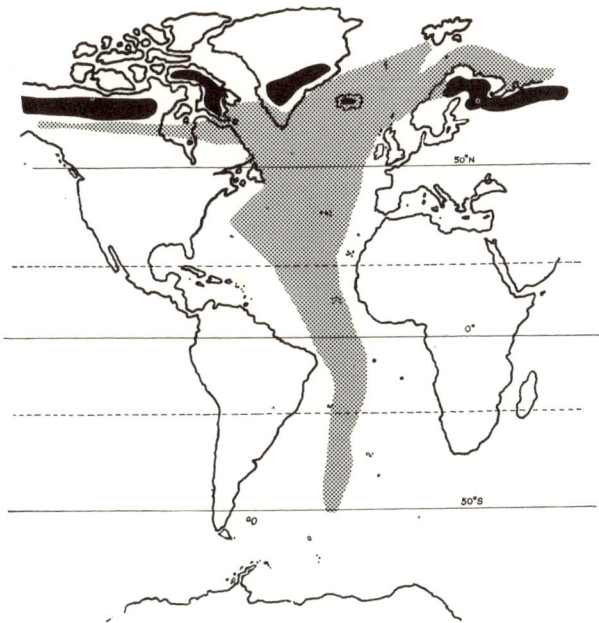 

When feeding in shallow water, phalaropes have a distinctive habit of spinning round – it is said to stir up food from the bottom – before up-ending like a duck.

In winter they wander far down over the ocean, in the Atlantic being recorded as far south as latitude 50°S.

WILSON'S PHALAROPE

Phalaropus tricolor

Wing span 17 inches.

This is the largest and least pelagic of the phalaropes. In fact it will very seldom be seen far out to sea; never in mid-ocean. It breeds fairly widely over the North American continent, even as far south as California, making the typical phalarope nest with four well-marked pointed eggs.

The female, in breeding plumage, has an almost flame-coloured neck and breast. A broad stripe runs back from the eye, extending to a point on the middle of the back. Through the eye, the stripe is black, but it gradually turns to rich chocolate as it comes aft. There is another rich chocolate bar running back beneath the first stripe from the shoulder. There is a white patch on either side of the eye-stripe. The belly is white and the back, apart from the banded portions, a delicate shade of grey. The legs are long and black. The bill is very slender, black and considerably longer than that of the other two phalaropes. The male is a smaller, untidy, drabber edition of the female.

In winter the birds may be seen at sea anywhere down the east coast of South America as far as the Falkland Islands; the sexes are alike, browny-grey on the back, white beneath and on the face they have a not very conspicuous grey eye-stripe.

RED-NECKED PHALAROPE

(Syn.: northern phalarope)

Phalaropus lobatus

Wing span 14 inches.

The female red-necked phalarope, with her brilliant chestnut-red neck and contrasting white throat patch, gives this species its English name. Her head is a rich blue-grey, her back striated gold and black. The male is less bright and rather smaller. His neck is a dull orange, the crown is duller and faintly blotchy, and he has a white face, which the female has not.

These, however, are breeding plumages and the ocean traveller will never see them thus. He will see the winter plumage, which is white beneath and striated black and grey above. There is a beautiful black eye-stripe. The bills of both sexes are the same, summer and winter; long, very slender, slightly down-curved and black.

The red-necked phalarope, in spite of its American

BIRDS OF THE ATLANTIC OCEAN

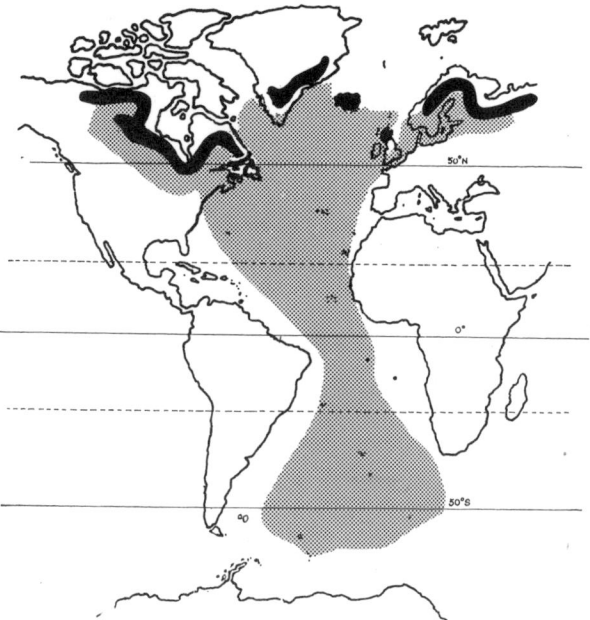

synonym, breeds slightly farther south than other members of the family. Its breeding grounds are still circum-polar, but extend as far south as Scandinavia, sub-Arctic Canada and the far north of the British Isles.

The boldly blotched, olive, pointed eggs – four of them – are laid in May or June.

In winter, the entire population moves away south across the ocean, taking up residence at sea anywhere between the equator and latitude 60°S.

1. Red-necked Phalarope (winter plumage).
2. Wilson's Phalarope (winter plumage).
3. Grey Phalarope (winter plumage).
4. Wilson's Phalarope (adult male spring plumage).
5. Wilson's Phalarope (adult female spring plumage).
6. Red-necked Phalarope (winter plumage).
7. Red-necked Phalarope (adult female spring plumage).
8. Grey Phalarope (winter plumage).   9. Sheathbill.
10. Grey Phalarope (adult female spring plumage).
11. Wilson's Phalarope (winter plumage).

FAMILY *CHIONIDIDAE* – SHEATHBILLS

SHEATHBILL
Chionis alba

Wing span 31 inches.

This is a strange bird of the far south. It is something of a scientific enigma as little is understood about its origin or its relation to other species.

It is a white bird with a horny bill, of pigeon-like appearance and size. It was known by Norwegian whalers as the 'ptarmigan'. It is, apparently, delicious to eat and so are its eggs, so there was, at one time, a distinct danger of its numbers being seriously depleted. Man's growing awareness, however, of the futility of wholesale destruction of wild birds may mean that it is now safe as a species.

The sheathbill is not an ocean bird; it is not a sea bird in any sense. But the fact that it is frequently seen many hundreds of miles from the nearest land, on ice flows, earns it a place in this book.

It is a scavenger of the first water and quite fearless of man. The tremendous increase of human activity in the Antarctic in recent years has shown that, wherever man with his attendant waste has set up camp, there the sheathbill will be too. The bird not only feeds on waste food and refuse, but on penguin droppings and eggs, on the placental blood of cubbing seals, on the placentas themselves, and on any waste matter. They have even been observed plucking at the umbilical cords of new-born seals before separation has occurred. In fact, the sheathbill is a wonderful, if somewhat macabre, demonstration of the fact that, in nature, nothing is wasted.

Sheathbills nest at the south of South Georgia, South Orkneys and other islands of the Antarctic archipeligo. They may be encountered anywhere south of latitude 65°S., in the region of the Straits of Magellan, in the Falkland Islands and up the southern part of the Patagonian coast.

The nests are built among large stones usually not far from the water. They are composed of grass, moss, feathers, waste food and other refuse. Three

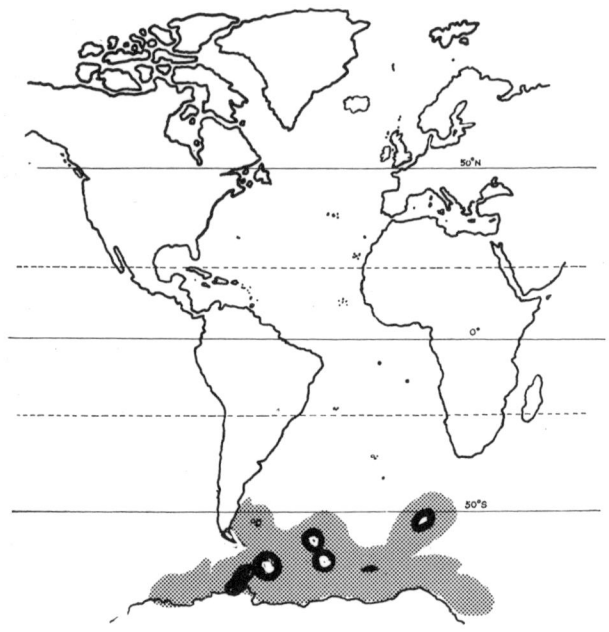

boldly brown-blotched, dirty-white eggs, which are often liberally freckled with black or brown, are laid in December at intervals of more than a week. As incubation starts when the first egg is laid, only one chick usually survives. Incubation takes twenty-eight days and the young bird is fledged a month from hatching.

Sheathbills, when courting or when 'barnyarding' around the habitations of man, behave astonishingly like the pigeons they resemble. They strut and mince around in circles, bobbing and bowing and cooing for all the world as if they were in Trafalgar Square, on the steps of St Paul's or in the Piazza San Marco.

FAMILY *STERCORARIIDAE* – SKUAS

Skuas are closely related to gulls and resemble them in general shape, though not in particulars. Strong flying, long winged and rather more oceanic than gulls, they are scavengers and predators of considerable courage and viciousness. Predation, in the case of the skua, consists mostly of attacking other sea birds and making them disgorge. The food thus released is then followed with great dash and frequently caught before it even reaches the sea. Being excellent fliers they harass gulls and cormorants. They also feed on carrion and, during the nesting season, on the eggs and young of other birds.

Characteristic features of the family are the hooked bill consisting of four horny layers, the generally dark plumage, the long central tail feathers, and the sharply angled wings.

They are, for the most part, birds of high Arctic latitudes. Outside the breeding season, they wander considerable distances, Arctic-breeding birds penetrating far into the southern hemisphere.

There are Antarctic skuas, too, but these do not wander further north than the temperate zones of the southern hemisphere.

Skuas defend their nests with great ferocity and have frequently been known to strike human as well as other intruders. A walk in the vicinity of a colony of nesting skuas can be quite an alarming experience.

The three smaller species in this family are dimorphic, having dark phase and light phase individuals.

POMARINE SKUA

(Syn.: pomatorhine skua, pomarine jaeger)

Stercorarius pomarinus

Wing span 48 inches.

This is a very easily recognised member of the skua family. Similar to the Arctic skua in colouring, but an altogether heavier bird, with two central tail feathers, spoon-ended and twisted, giving the tail a curious bulbous-ended appearance which is discernible a long way off.

In light phase, the bird is ashy-brown on its back with a pale band at the base of the primaries. It has a white belly, a grey-brown chest band, black cap and face with lemon-yellow cheeks. The feet are black. The vicious, hooked bill is pale yellow, and black tipped.

Dark phase birds are uniformly ashy-brown all over but otherwise similar. Immature birds are pale, mottled stripy-brown and buff, and the central tail feathers extend only a short way.

The bird breeds in widely scattered colonies on the islands and coasts of the Arctic Ocean. It winters at sea, frequenting off-shore fishing banks and the fishing grounds of shearwaters. It has been seen as far south as Gibraltar on the eastern side of the Atlantic and off Florida on the western side. Greater numbers are reported from the west, although this bird is essentially pelagic in its wanderings and is

BIRDS OF THE ATLANTIC OCEAN

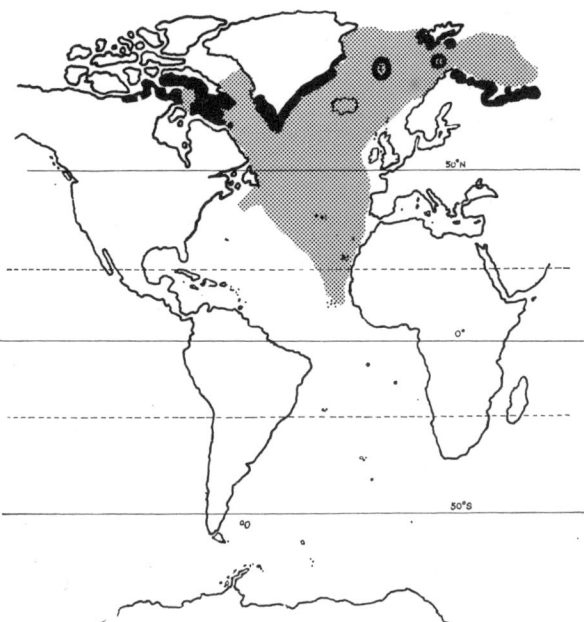

seldom, if ever, seen from land. The bird's call is described as a squealing, hawk-like whistle. Two olive eggs, very sparingly spotted with brown, are laid on the ground in a grass-lined cup, in June. Rarely, nests are on cliff ledges.

1. Pomarine Skua (dark phase). 2. Pomarine Skua (light phase). 3. Great Skua. 4. Long-tailed Skua. 5. Arctic Skua (immature). 6. Arctic Skua (adult dark phase).

ARCTIC SKUA

(Syn.: parasitic jaeger)

Stercorarius parasiticus

Wing span 41 inches.

The light phase of the Arctic skua is ashy-brown above, white beneath with a grey chest band, a black cap and lemon-white cheeks and neck. There is a pale band on the wings caused by the white quills of the primaries. In nearly every respect it is very similar to the pomarine skua, but is smaller and the two central tail feathers are extended but come to fine points.

The dark phase birds are a more uniform ashy-brown, but are markedly paler beneath. The young are mottled brown, without a black cap and with only very slightly extended central tail feathers.

The Arctic skua nests throughout the Arctic and well down into the higher temperate latitudes. Birds of either colour phase interbreed freely, but those which breed further south – those with nests in

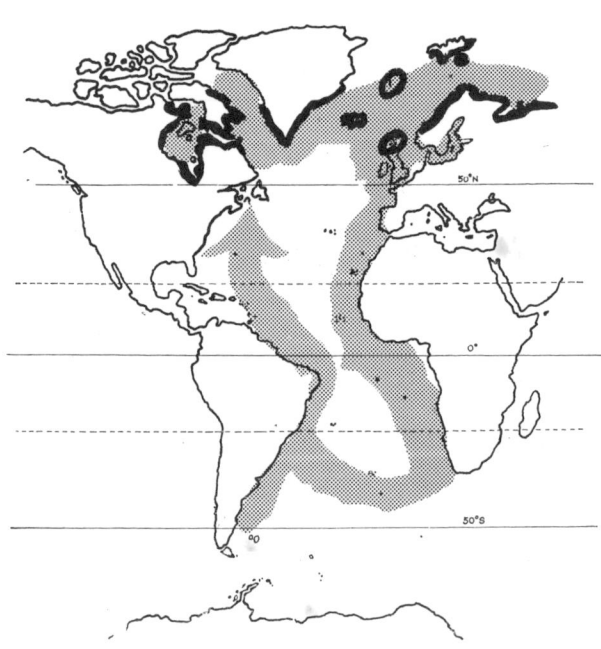

BIRDS OF THE ATLANTIC OCEAN

Scottish islands, temperate northern Europe and temperate Canada – are more frequently dark phase birds.

Two eggs are usually laid in June in a depression in the ground on grassy islands or on open moorland. The eggs are olive with a few dark markings. Nests in colonies are usually well separated and are fiercely defended.

The Arctic skua is a very swift and agile flier, capable of great manoeuvrability; it has to be for terns are its principal prey. It follows them, twisting and turning so that, try as they may to shake off their pursuer, they finally and inevitably surrender their catch.

In winter, Arctic skuas travel enormous distances across the oceans, sometimes following flocks of migrating terns. They also frequently visit harbours or inland waters and may be seen on either side of the Atlantic as far as the Argentine and the Cape of Good Hope.

When swimming they do so in a very buoyant, upright position which is clearly diagnostic.

LONG-TAILED SKUA

(Syn.: long-tailed jaeger)

Stercorarius longicaudus

Wing span 39 inches.

The smallest of the skuas, this bird is similar in colouring to the two previous species, but it has very greatly extended central tail feathers. They are, in fact, longer in relation to the bird than the swallow's extended outer tail feathers. The young bird, though it hasn't got the long tail, is distinguishable from other skuas by being a far paler, almost grey, mottled bird.

The long-tailed skua breeds in the very far north on the shores of the Arctic Ocean. The eggs, which are laid in July, are placed in a depression in the ground, usually at some height above sea level; sometimes even on the lower slopes of mountains. They are olive brown with darker, irregular markings.

Not much is known about the full winter range of this species, though it is known to wander well down into the southern oceans. It is seldom encountered at sea, but when it is, is often found to be in quite large concentrations.

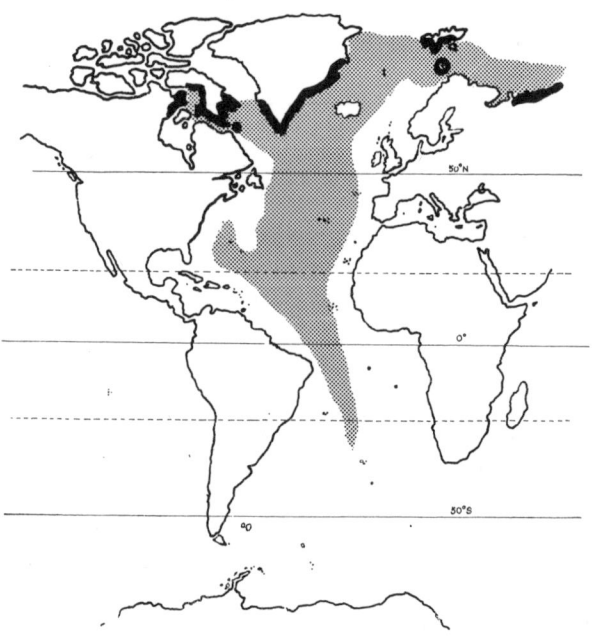

GREAT SKUA

(Syns: skua, bonxie)

Catharacta skua

Wing span 59 inches.

The great skua is one of the very few birds which have bi-polar distribution. Though the other members of the skua family are essentially Arctic birds, its distribution is divided, with a heavy numerical preponderance occurring in the Antarctic.

A far heavier bird than the other skuas, this species superficially resembles immature members of the larger gulls in shape and colour. It is a mottled brown and buff bird with a pale band at the base of the primaries. The tail is wedge-shaped and the two central feathers extend so little that they are not really noticeable except under close inspection. The legs are black and the bill is powerful and hooked.

The race, *C. skua*, gives the name to the super species; it being assumed that skuas are Arctic in origin. In the Antarctic, the cinnamon skua, *C. chilensis*, the southern skua, *C. antarctica*, and the dark skua, *C. lönnbergi*, have overlapping distribution. All are races of the super species and all are darker than the great skua by varying amounts.

In the north, skuas nest on Iceland, in Greenland and Labrador, on the Faroes and Shetland Islands. In the south, they nest on the Antarctic coasts and on Antarctic and sub-Antarctic islands. They lay two olive-brown eggs on open ground. Nests are in loose colonies. They are laid in June in the north and

ORDER *LARO-LIMICOLAE*

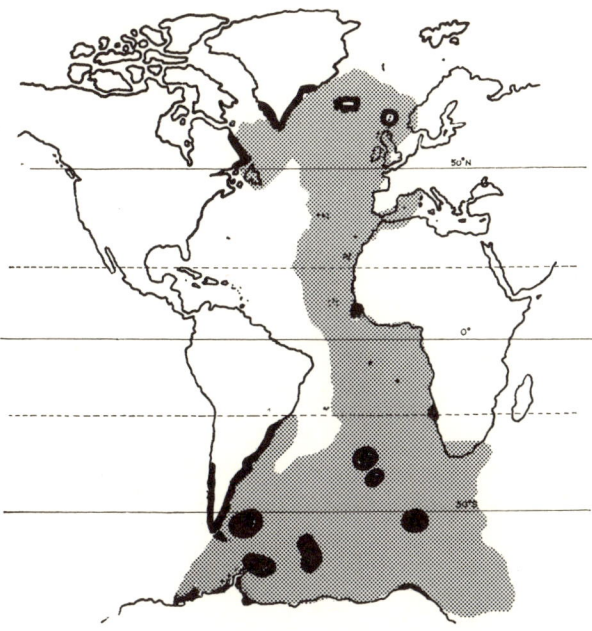

between September and January in the south, depending on location.

The skua is one of the fiercest and cruellest of all birds. It is a ruthless predator – a robber of other birds, a killer of the smaller and weaker ones and a voracious scavenger.

Out of the breeding season, the skuas of the north range southward almost to the Antarctic. They spend most of their time at sea, but may be seen around harbours and estuaries wherever there are large congregations of gulls and other sea birds. The skuas of the south are not recorded as wandering farther north than the temperate and sub-tropical zones of the South Atlantic.

BIRDS OF THE ATLANTIC OCEAN

FAMILY *LARIDAE*

It is surprising how few people realize what a large group of birds the gulls are. To most, a sea-gull is a sea-gull – or a 'seagle' as many sailors say. Ask the average seafaring man what sort of gulls were in such and such a place and he will look at you pityingly and say: 'Well just gulls; seagulls!' As a matter of fact, he is not so very far off the mark, for many of the different species are very closely related and it seems likely that, to make up the twenty-five recognised species of Atlantic gull, the original ancestral stock did not exceed more than about four recognizable super species.

Long-winged, streamlined and, for the most part, white birds with darker backs and, in some cases, darker heads, gulls are, with one exception, non-pelagic. They nest in the vicinity of the sea and spend a lot of their lives over the sea, but many also penetrate a long way inland. They are, however, essentially water birds, having webbed feet and the necessary oil glands to enable them to remain afloat indefinitely without their feathers becoming waterlogged.

They are Arctic in origin, though many have now established themselves in the south. With a few exceptions, they are predatory thieves. All are scavengers.

Sub-family *Larinae* – gulls

DOMINICAN GULL

(Syns: kelp gull, southern black-backed gull)
Larus dominicanus

Wing span 54 inches.

This is the only large black-backed gull to be found in the southern hemisphere. It is about the same size as the lesser black-backed gull of the northern waters, and very similar in colouring. The head, neck, tail and underparts are white; the mantle is sooty black. There are white tips to the wings. The bill is yellow with an orange spot on it and the legs are yellow. The young are mottled brown and white with black wing tips and tail, unlike the mature bird. The

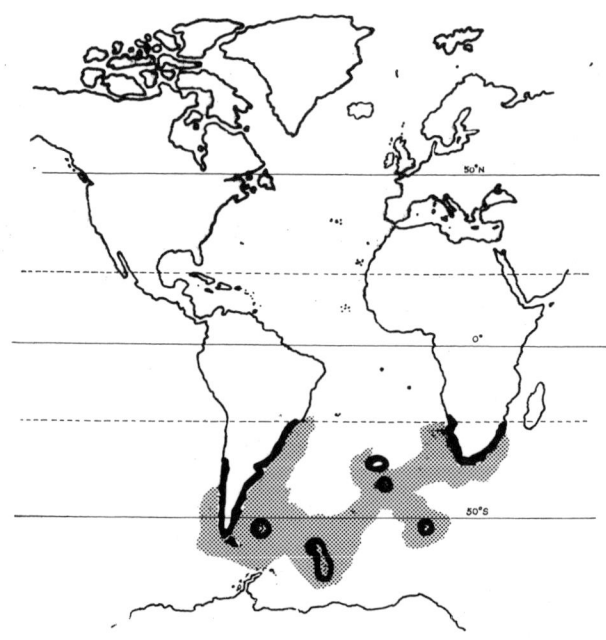

Herring Gull

young have a black bill and brown feet.

Kelp gulls occur in every southern ocean. In the Atlantic, they breed on the south African coast, on the South American coast as far north as Rio, and in most sub-Antarctic islands.

The eggs are large, pointed greenish with dark brown and black splodges. The nest is built of seaweed and other flotsam on flat ground or on cliff ledges. Eggs are laid from October to January depending on latitude.

The bird is a fierce predator, taking the eggs and young of any other bird, including its own species, and is a lover of any form of carrion.

GREAT BLACK-BACKED GULL

Larus marinus

Wing span 66 inches.

This, the largest gull in the world, is widespread in the northern hemisphere. Some north European individuals attain a wing span of close on six feet. The adult bird is white except for a jet-black mantle. The powerful bill is yellow with an orange spot and the feet are flesh-coloured.

It breeds on all Arctic and sub-Arctic coasts. Its nest is usually on flat ground on islets; always near the sea, but seldom on cliff ledges. Three olive-brown darkly splodged eggs are laid in April or May, possibly as late as July in the northern extremities of its range.

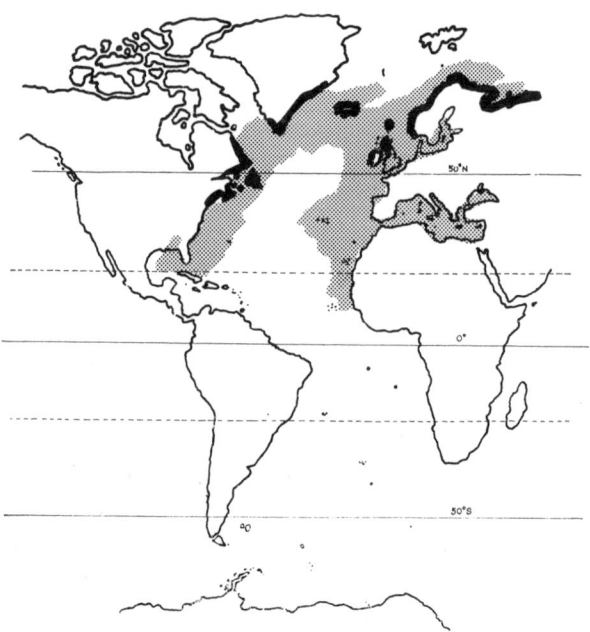

On the European side of the Atlantic, the bird is fairly solitary, though, when not breeding, it seems to have no objection to mixing in flocks with other gulls. On the American side, individual birds are noticeably smaller and they nest in colonies and are generally far more gregarious.

Immature great black-backs are brown and white mottled with dark brown wing tips and tail. They look larger than adult birds, but this is an illusion caused partly by different colour and partly by plumage which in the greater disarray of immaturity is rather more fluffed out.

They are, like most gulls, ruthless predators. Their size, however, makes them more destructive than most. They prey on the eggs and young of ducks, particularly eiders, of cormorants, terns and other gulls. They take adults of smaller species, including petrels, guillemots and puffins. They rob other members of their family and eat carrion and general refuse. There are nearly always one or two great black-backs among the other gulls which daily congregate around large refuse dumps.

GLAUCOUS GULL

Larus hyperboreus

Wing span 62 inches.

The glaucous gull is almost as large as the great black-back. In fact, the larger individuals of this species may exceed the size of the western Atlantic great black-back gulls. It is a white gull with very pale grey mantle and white wing tips. The bill is long and heavy; yellow with orange spots. The legs and feet are a very pale flesh-colour.

Young birds are mottled creamy-buff and brown; paler than most other immature gulls. They have a whitish bill with a dark tip. They take four years to attain full adult plumage.

The glaucous gull is, as near as makes no difference, a pure bird of prey. It will capture adult auks and plovers on the wing as well as robbing other birds of their eggs and young. It frequently swallows its prey whole, feathers and all. At other times it will hold its catch under one foot like an eagle and tear it to bloody shreds.

It nests on most Arctic coasts in colonies on cliff ledges or on high islets, often in the vicinity of guillemot or razorbill colonies. Three pale brown eggs, liberally marked with dark brown are laid in a nest of moss and seaweed anytime from May to July.

In winter, these gulls wander as far south as

ORDER *LARO-LIMICOLAE*

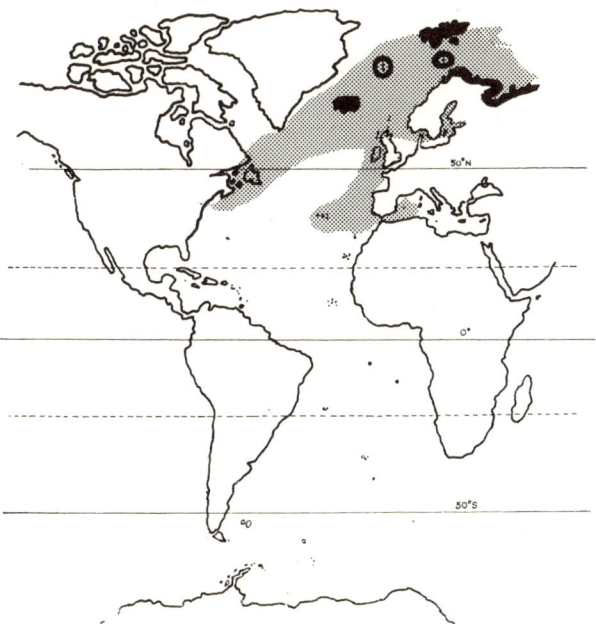

There is no doubt, however, that they are all very closely related and probably stem from the same ancestral source. Not only are they very closely related, but, within each species, there is so much geographical and racial variation, that it is sometimes very difficult to pin them down. And when it comes to recognising immature birds, a stranger in the area can only ask advice from local ornithologists.

Thayer's gull, now accepted as a distinct species, is a gull of northern Arctic Canada; breeding from the west coast of Greenland north and west. It ranges down the Pacific coast of Canada out of the breeding season, so will only be seen on the Atlantic side of Canada in the summer and then not south of the Davis strait.

It is very similar to the herring gull; white with pale grey mantle, yellow bill with orange spot, flesh-coloured legs, but the wing tips are white.

Virginia in the west and Gibraltar in the east. They are, however, seldom seen around the British Isles as they move south farther out to sea. They tend to congregate around fishing banks.

THAYER'S GULL

Larus thayeri

Wing span 56 inches.

We now come to a group of four gulls which are, at the moment, recognised as four separate species.

ICELAND GULL

(Syn.: Kumlien's gull)

Larus glaucoides

Wing span 54 inches.

This gull, a close relation of the herring gull, is similar in colour to the glaucous gull; white with pale grey mantle and white wing tips. The wings, however, are longer and more slender in proportion to the size of bird. It has a graceful and buoyant flight.

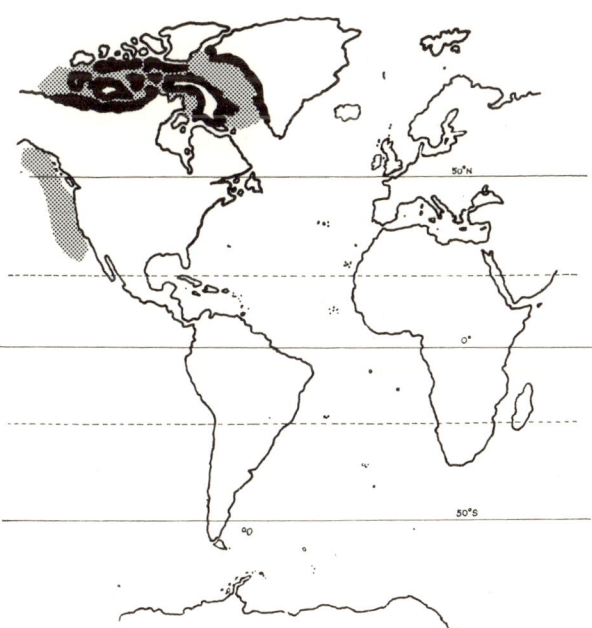

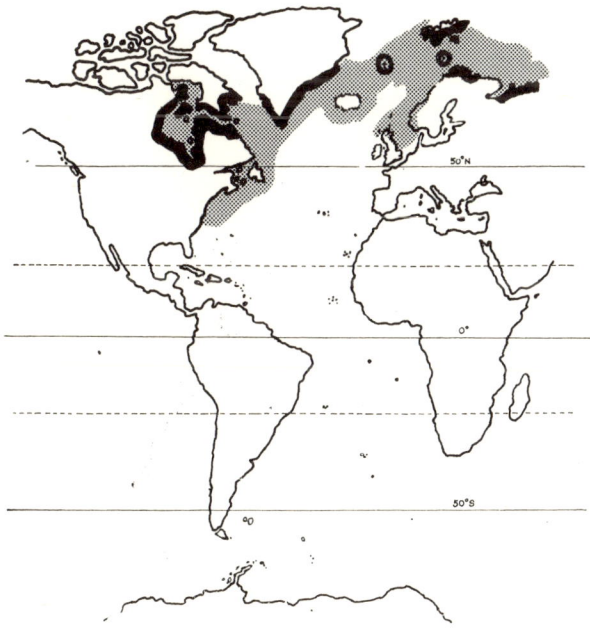

BIRDS OF THE ATLANTIC OCEAN

It is not such a vicious bird of prey as the glaucous gull, though it resembles its closer relatives in feeding habits, being a master scavenger and inveterate thief.

It breeds on the Arctic islands of North America, on the cliffs of Greenland, Jan Mayen Island, Novaya Zemlya and northern Siberia. Two to three eggs, which are greenish brown with dark splodges, are laid in a typical gull nest of moss and seaweed, on cliff ledges, any time from May to July.

Iceland gulls may be seen on open coastal waters in winter as far south as New York in the west and Brittany in the east.

HERRING GULL

Larus argentatus

Wing span 56 inches.

This is probably the best known gull of the northern Atlantic Ocean. There are, however, many racial and geographical variations in the superficial colouring and details of the species. The north European bird is a large, white, elegant bird with a strong buoyant flight. It has a blue-grey mantle, yellow beak with orange spot and flesh-coloured legs. The wing tips are jet-black with well marked, contrasting white mirrors.

The North American bird, *L.a. smithsonianus*, is not so cleanliness contrasting. In fact it is paler, drabber and slightly larger.

1. Lesser Black-backed Gull.   2. Iceland Gull.
3. Common Gull (winter plumage).   4. Common Gull.
5. Great Black-backed Gull.   6. Glaucous Gull.
7. Andouin's Gull.   8. Dominican Gull.   9. Thayer's Gull.
10. Ring-billed Gull.   11. Ring-billed Gull (winter plumage).

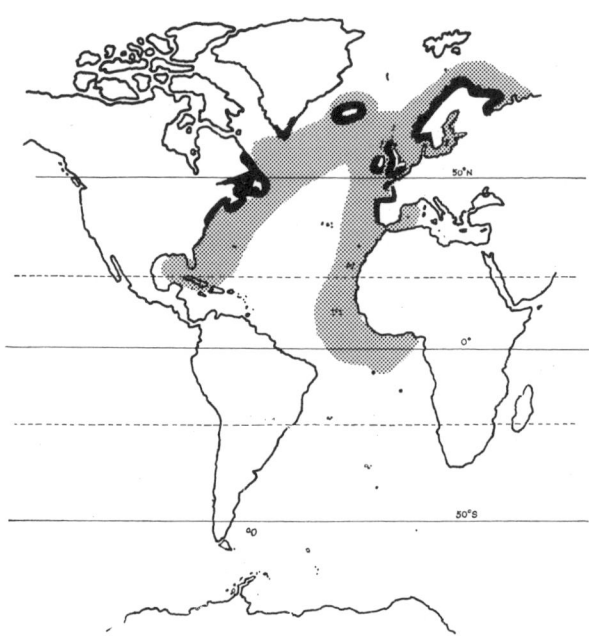

The Scandinavian and Mediterranean herring gulls of the race *omissus* and *cachinnans* have yellow legs. *Cachinnans* has a dark grey mantle. There is every conceivable combination of the above variations in between. It is, therefore, very difficult – almost impossible – to draw the line where the herring gull ends and the lesser black-backed gull starts.

Herring gulls have a variety of the most musical calls. The noise, in the vicinity of their cliff nesting sites at the height of the breeding season resembles a pack of foxhounds in full cry. There is a hard, gutteral *'tuk, tuk, tuk,'* a loud and repeated *'kyoo'*, which is the cry of alarm and anger, and a long, drawn-out, cat-like mew.

It is one of the most evil scoundrels of all birds. It feeds on rubbish, waste food, other birds' eggs, other birds' young; even, if the slightest pressed, its own young. Nothing is too despicable for the herring gull in its battle for survival – a surprisingly successful battle considering the infamy of the creature!

Nests are built of seaweed and flotsam on most

North Atlantic coasts. Sometimes they are more readily accessible on flat ground, sometimes on coastal cottages, but more often, on cliff ledges. Three, sometimes four, brown or green, well-marked and pointed eggs are laid anytime from April to August. The young are mottled brown and buff with browny-black beaks, legs, tail and wing tips. They do not attain full adult plumage until about five years old.

When not breeding herring gulls can be seen in the vicinity of every north Atlantic coast line as far south as Panama and central Africa. They frequently move inland for great distances in search of food, like frogs, grubs, worms, beetles and, favourite of all, garbage.

LESSER BLACK-BACKED GULL

Larus fuscus

Wing span 58 inches.

So closely related is this species to the previous one that it is difficult to understand fully why it has been specifically separated. From a British standpoint, however, there is absolutely no doubt about the difference between the two birds. The lesser black-back is slightly larger than the herring gull and has a sooty black mantle and yellow legs. It is markedly smaller than the great black-back and the mantle is not as jet black. Scandinavian lesser black-backs do, however, have jet-black backs. The most certain diagnostic difference when size is difficult to judge, between the two species, however, is in the legs; lesser black-backs are rich yellow, great black-backs are pale flesh-colour.

The eggs and immature birds are similar to those of the herring gull, but the lesser black-back tends to lay more on the ground than on cliff ledges. The bird breeds only on the eastern side of the Atlantic.

Out of the breeding season lesser black-backs wander farther south than herring gulls and practically disappear from the shores of northern Europe. Though they do not breed on the American side of the Atlantic, increasing numbers have been seen there in recent years. On the Maine coast, for instance, where great black-backed gulls abound, the lesser black-back is readily spotted by its yellow legs and has been seen in small numbers even during the summer in recent years.

COMMON GULL

(Syn.: mew gull)

Larus canus

Wing span 44 inches.

The name, common gull, is misleading. It is doubtful whether the total world population of this gull is as great as that of the herring gull and its near relatives.

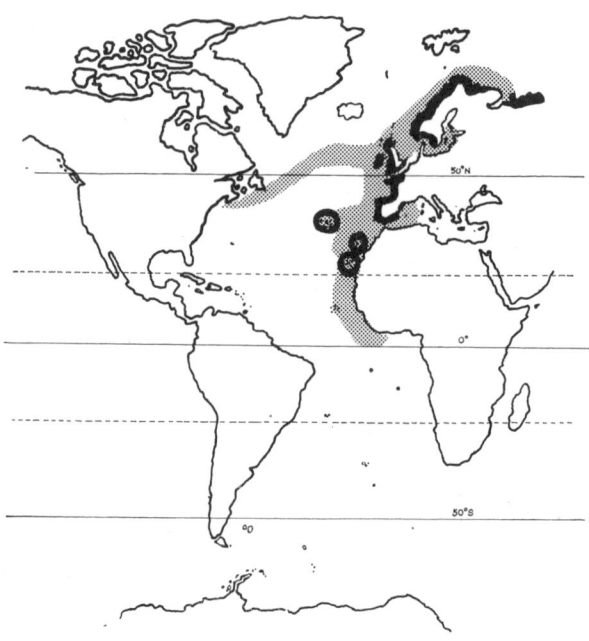
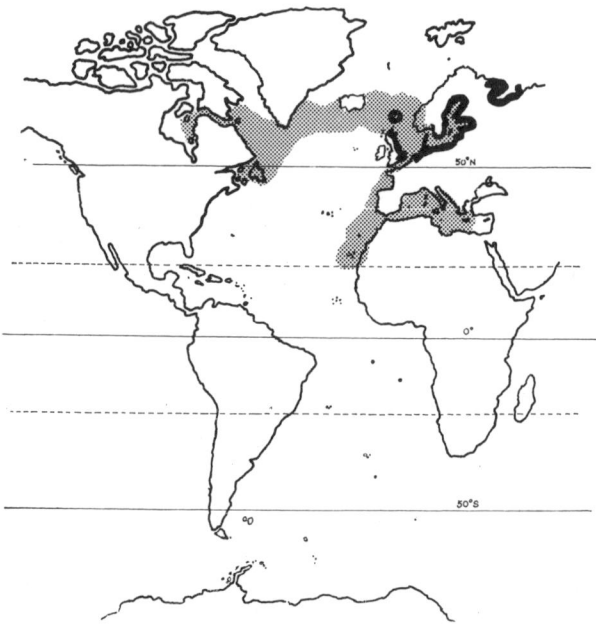

ORDER *LARO-LIMICOLAE*

As far as the British Isles and North America are concerned it is certainly not nearly as common. But in Denmark and other low-lying, grassy lands of northern Europe it is very numerous; 500,000 pairs were counted in Denmark alone about twenty years ago.

It is similar in colour to the herring gull, white with grey mantle and black wing tips with white mirrors. The bill, however, is far more slender and is plain yellow without the orange spots, and the legs are greenish. The immature bird is white beneath, has a slightly grey-dappled head, a white tail with a black bar across it and a mottled brown and buff back. Adult birds have slight grey streaks on their heads when out of breeding plumage.

Common gulls nest on marshy ground or on pebbles, sometimes even on cliffs and hillsides, near either salt or fresh water. Colonies are usually small and birds do nest singly. The eggs are paler than the large gulls' eggs, café-au-lait colour spotted with brown, and are laid in May, June or July.

Common gulls are as terrestial as they are marine and travel great distances inland, sometimes in mixed flocks with other gulls, to feed on earth-worms and grubs – particularly those turned up at ploughing time.

As the slender, almost plover-like bill of this bird suggests, its habits are far less barbarous than those of the larger gulls. It is still, however, not averse to stealing an egg or two from its neighbours.

Great Lakes on islands in lakes, in marshy country, on cliffs and maritime hillsides. It has even been recorded nesting in low trees.

Three buff eggs with brown markings are laid in May or June.

In winter, ring-billed gulls spread southward, reaching Cuba and Mexico, and sometimes as far out in the ocean as Bermuda.

RING-BILLED GULL

Larus delawarensis

Wing span 48 inches.

This is probably the commonest gull in North America. It is a white bird, smaller than the herring gull, but rather larger than the common gull, having a similar grey back to both, with white-mirrored black wing tips. It has bright yellow legs. The distinguishing mark, as the name implies, is a dark, almost black, ring around the bill about two-thirds of the way out.

Immature birds, though mottled like other young gulls, are not uniformly brown. The head soon becomes almost white – within the first year. The tail feathers are white except for an even black band across them, near the tip. The end third of the bill is well-defined black.

It is a fresh as well as a sea water bird, and nests right across the American continent north of the

AUDOUIN'S GULL

Larus audouinii

Wing span 42 inches.

This is a comparitively rare gull, found only in the Mediterranean. The adult bird has white head, underparts and tail. The mantle is grey and the wing tips are black with white mirrors. The legs are dark grey. The bill is bright red with a black band across it near the tip.

In winter, the adult Audouin's gull's beak is streaked with grey.

Immature birds are mottled brown and are distinguishable from the young of other gulls in the same region, only by their smaller size.

Three olive-buff eggs with dark, irregular markings are laid at the end of April or the beginning of May, either on the ground or on cliff ledges. The bird breeds on parts of the Spanish coast, in Sardinia and Corsica, in Tunisia and Syria.

BIRDS OF THE ATLANTIC OCEAN

It is fairly easily seen in nearly every part of the Mediterranean when out of the breeding season.

DOLPHIN GULL
(Syn.: Magellan gull)

Larus scoresbii

Wing span 40 inches.

The dolphin gull is another gull which is largely terrestrial. It is entirely confined to the extreme southern end of the Atlantic and also occurs on the South American Pacific coast.

It is a black-backed gull, though the contrast between the black mantle and the rest of the bird is not so marked, as the head, neck and underparts are pale grey, not white. The under surface of the wings is dark grey. The bill and legs are red. The only white on the bird is the tail and the tips of the wings. In winter the head is dusky.

Immature birds have a dark brown mantle, pale brown head, neck and breast, and yellowish-white underparts. The tail is white with a broad black bar across the end of it.

The bird breeds on the Patagonian coast, on Tierra del Fuego and the Falkland Islands. Eggs are laid in December and January.

Outside the breeding season the bird may be seen in the vicinity of the Straits of Magellan, up the coast of South America as far as Montevideo, and around

Immature Gulls: 1. Glaucous Gull.
2. Iceland Gull (second winter plumage).
3. Glaucous Gull (second summer plumage).
4. Lesser Black-backed Gull. 5. Herring Gull.
6. Great Black-backed Gull. 7. Dominican Gull.
8. Common Gull. 9. Herring Gull (second summer plumage).
10. Ring-billed Gull.

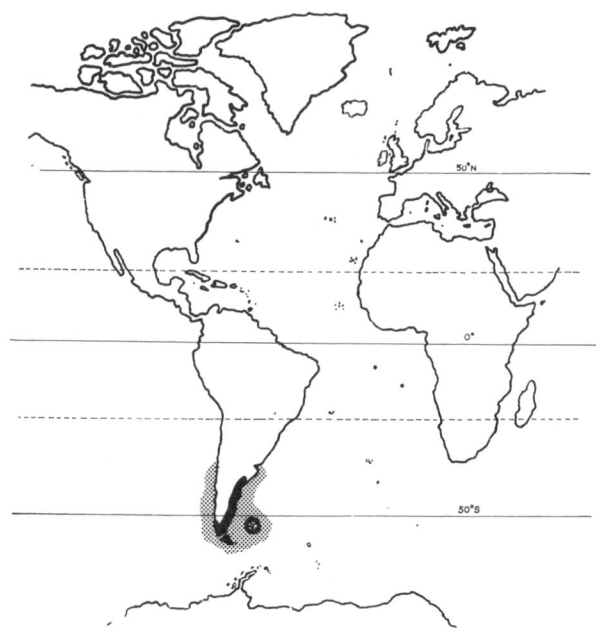

BIRDS OF THE ATLANTIC OCEAN

all the sub-Antarctic islands in that quarter of the ocean.

GREAT BLACK-HEADED GULL

Larus (Ichthyaëtus) ichthyaëtus

Wing span 54 inches.

Almost as large as the herring gull, this is by far the largest of the so called black-headed gulls. Its head is, in fact, true black – not chocolate – in summer, except for white crescents above and below the eye. The rest of the bird is white with a grey mantle and black, mirrored wing tips. The bill is very sturdy; yellow with a black band near the tip. The legs and feet are greenish yellow. In winter – and it is only in winter that the bird will be seen at sea – the head loses its black plumage. It becomes a dull white with dusky streaks.

Immature birds are pale mottled brown with a dark brown mantle. The rump, underparts and tail are white; the tail having a broad black band across it. The bill is black and the legs and feet dark grey.

Although this is the only large gull with a dark hood, it will be seen that recognition is not so easy at sea as the bird will rarely be seen in breeding plumage. Points to look for are the colouring of the bill and feet.

These gulls nest in south-east Russia and central Asia, but visit the Mediterranean in the winter. They have even been recorded as far afield as England.

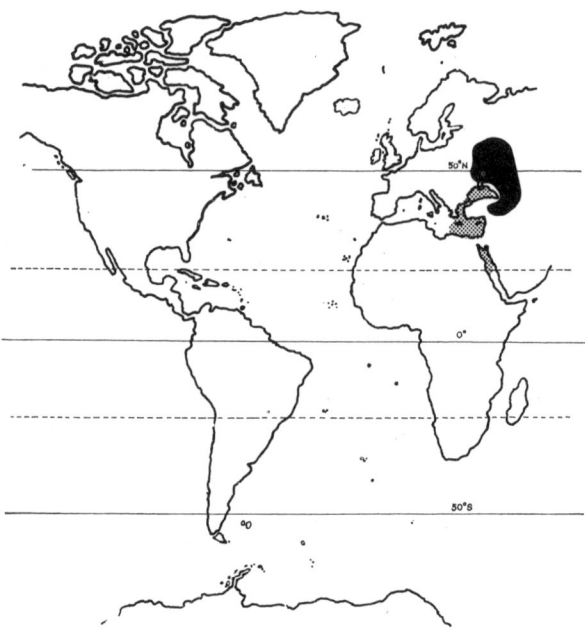

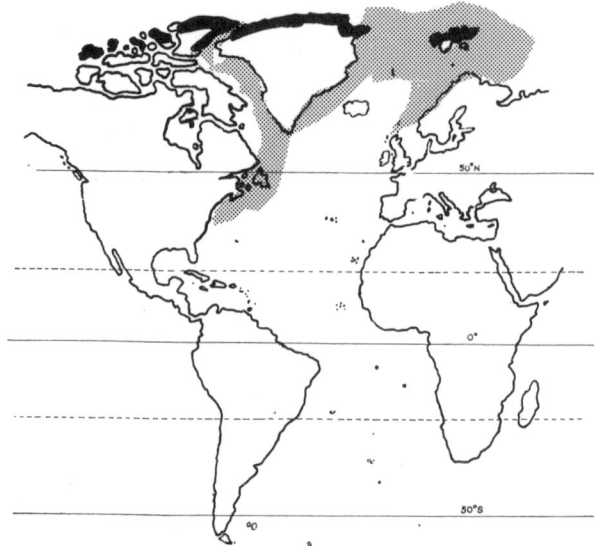

IVORY GULL

Larus (Pagophila) eburneus

Wing span 36 inches.

A pure white gull with rather short black legs and yellow bill, seen in the Arctic Ocean, can only be an ivory gull. Unlike most gulls, they seldom alight on the water, but are very active, running hither and thither, on ice or on land. They feed mostly on small mammals, insects and shell-fish. They also follow seals, whales and wolves to eat from their droppings. Like other gulls, they are scavengers, and attend on Eskimo hunters to glean flesh and blubber waste.

They breed in Greenland, Spitzbergen and other Arctic islands. Usually, the nest is on the ground, but may be on low cliff ledges. Two eggs are laid in a moss and lichen nest in July. They are olive buff with brown markings.

Immature birds have dusky faces and black bills. In winter, ivory gulls move southward and may be seen off the North American continent as far south as New England or off northern Europe as far south as France.

SABINE'S GULL

Larus (Xema) sabini

Wing span 30 inches.

Forked tails are usually associated with terns, a sub-family of the gull tribe. Sabine's gull, however, is one of two gulls – the swallow-tailed gull of the

ORDER *LARO-LIMICOLAE*

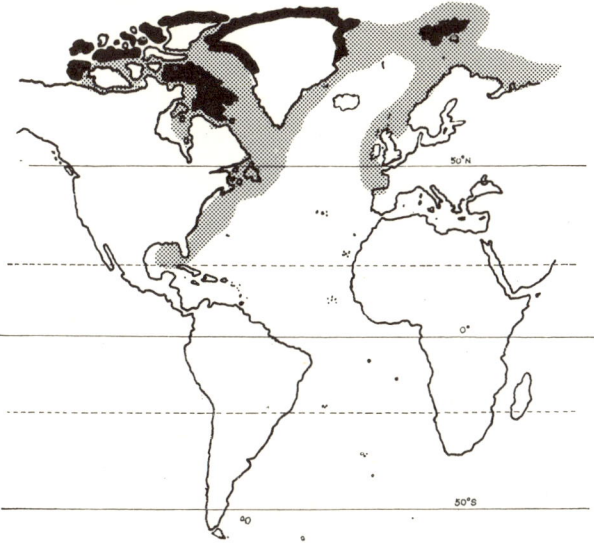

Pacific is the other – which have definite forked tails. It is a small gull of Arctic circum-polar breeding range, with slate-coloured head and throat when in breeding plumage. The underparts and the tail are white and the mantle is pearl grey and white, forming a distinct triangular pattern. The wing tips are black and white, and the bill and feet are dark; nearly black. In winter the head loses its grey colour and becomes just dirty white.

Immature birds are brown above and white beneath. The tail has a terminal black bar across it and the feet are brown.

Breeding in Alaska, north Canada, Greenland, Spitzbergen and northern Siberia, the bird wanders south in winter and may be seen as far south as France, Bermuda or Texas. It may be seen singly, but sometimes mass flights occur down each main continental coastline.

The eggs, olive brown and palely spotted, are laid in a hollow in damp ground from May to July.

ROSS'S GULL

Larus (Rhodostethia) roseus

Wing span 24 inches.

A very small gull which is rarely seen, Ross's gull has been something of a mystery until very recently. In breeding plumage – and very few people get an opportunity of seeing it thus – it has a white head with a black collar. The eyelids are a brilliant red. The back is pearly grey with black at the wing tips. Under the wings is grey. The underparts, rump and tail are rosy white. The bill is black and the feet red.

In winter, the black collar disappears. The immature bird has brownish-black crown, neck and mantle. The forehead and cheeks are dull white with a darker spot behind the eye. There is a dark bar on the back and a broad black terminal band on the otherwise completely white tail. The feet are pale plum colour.

Ross's gull is a fresh water breeder. The three eggs – laid in June – are green with brown spots usually placed on a substantial nest of sticks and grass close to the water.

Breeding grounds are very rarely found as the birds spread widely over the vast empty spaces of the Arctic when they are breeding.

LITTLE GULL

Larus (Hydrocoloeus) minutus

Wing span 21 inches.

Frequently seen flying and fishing with terns, this, the smallest of all the gulls, can easily be distinguished from them by its shorter, rounded wings. Nevertheless, it is still a buoyant, graceful, tern-like flier and fishes by diving on its prey in much the same manner as a tern.

In breeding plumage, the little gull has a deep chocolate – almost black – head, a pearl grey mantle with white edges to the wings, a red bill and red feet. The body and tail are white, but the underside of the wings are a deep grey, shading from almost black at the tips to dull, pale grey at the base. In winter, the 'black' head goes and there is a brown

BIRDS OF THE ATLANTIC OCEAN

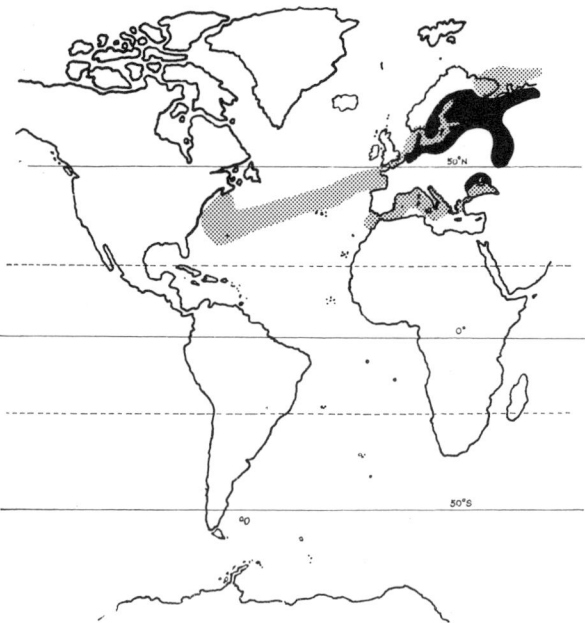

Immature Gulls: 1. Ivory Gull. 2. Little Gull.
3. Dolphin Gull. 4. Bonaparte's Gull.
5. Sabine's Gull. 6. Black-headed Gull. 7. Ross's Gull.
8. Black-headed Gull (adult winter plumage).

hood across the crown and a distinct brown spot behind each eye.

Immature birds have a dark brown bar across the end of the tail feathers, the winter head-pattern of the adult bird and a dark W on the back, the outside points of which are the wing tips, the base points are at the crank of the wing and the centre point is at the rump. In the triangle formed by the centre of the W there is a brown and buff striped mantle which terminates at the fore-end in a distinct brown half yoke across the base of the neck.

Little gulls nest in colonies on marshy ground north-east from Holland, through Sweden to Siberia. Three pale, olive-brown eggs which have darker splodges are laid in May or June.

In winter the birds spread to most European waters, to the Mediterranean and the Black Sea. They are only occasional visitors to the British Isles and to Bermuda and the east coast of the American continent.

It has not yet been established that any have ever bred in America, though some ornithologists think that this might well be possible.

BLACK-HEADED GULL

Larus (Chroicocephalus) ridibundus

Wing span 36 inches.

In any quiet, cold winter evening, in almost any river valley in Europe, huge skeins of gulls can be seen moving steadily towards the sea; high up in beautiful lines and Vee formations. And it will be noticeable that the nearer to the sea the greater and larger the formations of gulls.

In the morning, the same thing occurs in the opposite direction. The gulls are moving inland to pastures, ponds, lakes and streams, rich with the vast variation of grubs and garbage which make up their varied diet.

When the wind blows strongly the gulls fly low in rather ragged groups. But whichever way they travel, the numbers have, in recent years, become greater and greater until now a vast concourse of these gulls makes these beautiful diurnal journeys.

BIRDS OF THE ATLANTIC OCEAN

The vast majority of these gulls are black-headed gulls. Herring gulls, common gulls and great black-back gulls join in, sometimes flying in formation with the black-headed gulls, but their number is small.

The head of this graceful, gregarious and argumentative bird is a rich chocolate in the breeding season. The black-tipped, pearl-grey mantle has a distinctive frontal white wedge at the outer end. The underside of the wings is a smoky-grey; bill, legs and feet are coral red.

Immature birds are striated brown on their backs and have no more than a pale brown crown and a smudge behind the eye. In winter, the adult birds lose their 'black' heads, retaining only a dark crescent smudge behind the eye.

Immature birds have yellow legs and feet, and an orange bill with dark tip.

They breed in enormous colonies on the ground, among sand-dunes, on swampy ground, on seaside swards, on any deserted flats by fresh or salt water. The nests are built from the stems of aquatic vegetation and are placed close to each other.

Three brown eggs with black markings are laid at the end of April, but colonies which are accessible to man are usually harvested until June. The birds appear to be quite unconcerned and, provided they have not started incubating, continue to lay in the same nest.

The eggs are very good to eat and are sold in many European capitals as a delicacy.

The black-headed gull is one of the few birds who have really benefited by the onward (or is it backward?) march of civilization. Man's ever increasing

1. Ivory Gull.   2. Little Gull.   3. Dolphin Gull.
4. Bonaparte's Gull.
5. Sabine's Gull.   6. Black-headed Gull.
7. Ross's Gull (adult summer plumage).
8. Ross's Gull (adult winter plumage).

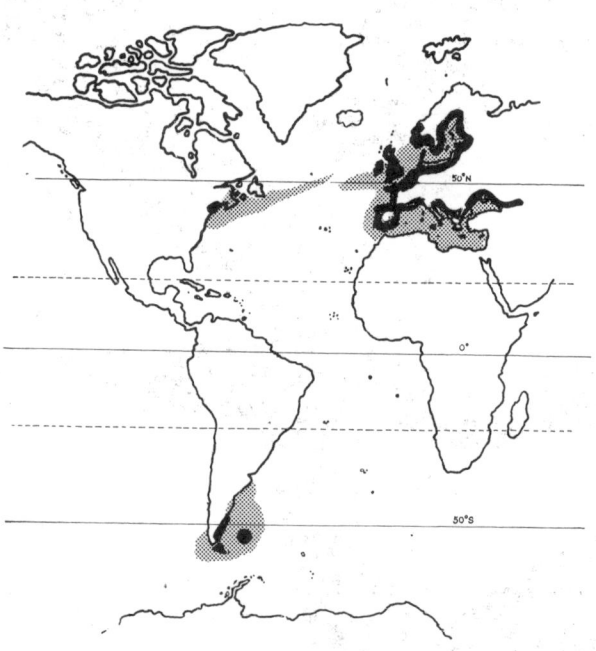

production of waste and garbage suits the bird's stomach so does man's ever increasing effort to grow the last ounce of food from every available acre of land. And what suits a bird's stomach suits its rate of reproduction and consequently the population has increased.

The black-headed gull is beneficial to agriculture; for it destroys insect pests, grubs and worms in the fields and often picks caterpillars from trees.

A few black-headed gulls have now spread to the North American continent, where they mingle with flocks of Bonaparte's gulls, and it cannot be long before there is large scale colonisation there, too.

There is, however, a race of the northern black-headed gull which may be seen on the eastern coasts of South America. The race, *maculipennis,* is very similar to *ridibundus,* but has a rosy hue underneath.

BIRDS OF THE ATLANTIC OCEAN

Birds of this race breed in the Falkland Islands, on Tierra del Fuego and in Patagonia.

BONAPARTE'S GULL

Larus (Chroicocephalus) philadelphia

Wing span 32 inches.

It is extraordinary that this dumpy little American gull, which, in many ways, is so similar to the black-headed gull, seems to be declining in population. Its habits, both flying and feeding, seem to be closely parallel out of the breeding season, but it does not breed in such concentrated colonies, and it usually nests in trees rather than on the ground.

In appearance it is similar to, though smaller than, the black-headed gull. The head, however, is dark grey in the breeding season as opposed to chocolate brown. Immature birds have a brown Vee of striated plumage on the back where the young of the black-head gull is more uniformly mottled brown. The bill of adult and young bird is deep grey, almost black, and compared with other gulls, very small and delicate.

Possibly the fact that they do not nest in such concentrated colonies has some affect on the population. It is known that colonial breeders are subjected to greater reproductive stimulation than solitary breeders.

Bonaparte's gulls nest in fir trees which are some-

1. Mediterranean Gull. 2. Mediterranean Gull (immature).
3. Mediterranean Gull (winter plumage). 4. Franklin's Gull.
5. Great Black-headed Gull.
6. Great Black-headed Gull (winter plumage).
7. Franklin's Gull (winter plumage).
8. Franklin's Gull (immature).
9. Great Black-headed Gull (immature).

times low, or sometimes high, around most of the lakes and marshes of Canada. In winter, they spread south and may be seen along the eastern American seaboard from New England to Florida.

SLENDER-BILLED GULL

Larus (Chroicocephalus) geneï

Wing span 34 inches.

A bird of south-west Europe, north-west Africa, the Mediterranean and the Black Sea, the slender-billed gull closely resembles the black-headed gull, but even when immature this gull has a white head. It is, in fact, a slightly heavier bird, though the wing span is marginally less.

It breeds in Spain, Asia Minor, Egypt and the coasts of the Black Sea. The nests are in colonies on

BIRDS OF THE ATLANTIC OCEAN

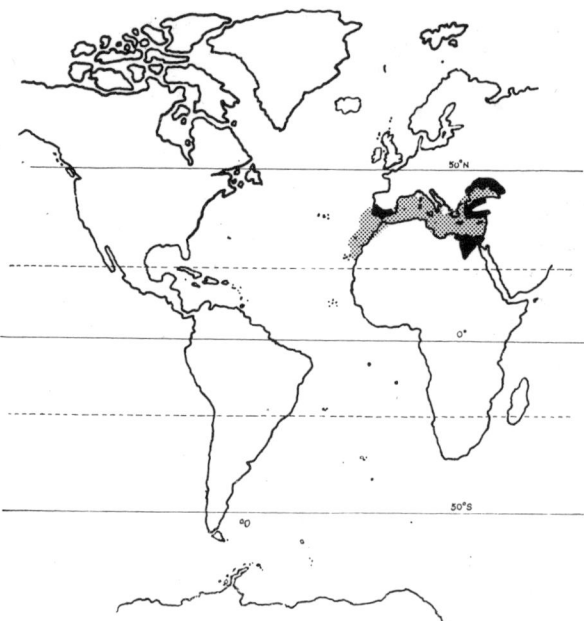

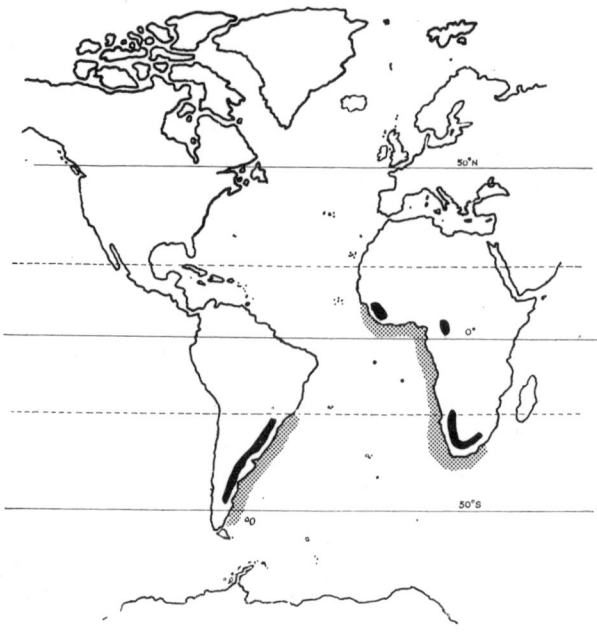

the ground and eggs are laid from April to July. Out of the breeding season, it may be seen on most Mediterranean and north-west African coasts.

Immature birds have a pale brown mantle, grey marks on the head and neck, a bar across the tail, orange bills, and yellow legs and feet.

GREY-HEADED GULL

Larus (Chroicocephalus) cirrhocephalus

Wing span 42 inches.

In the same way as the tubenoses are basically birds of the southern hemisphere, but have in a few instances settled in the northern hemisphere, so gulls are of northern origin and some have spread to the southern limits of the oceans. The grey-headed gull is one of these southern ocean gulls.

A medium-sized bird, it is distinguished from the black-headed gull by its grey, not chocolate, hood. It is slightly larger too. The grey hood extends to the throat and is thus more complete than the brown hood of *maculipennis*. Immature birds are almost indistinguishable from young black-headed gulls except by direct comparison of size.

They breed inland in South America and in tropical Africa, but may be seen on the coasts of either continent in winter. In winter, adult birds retain a considerable proportion of their grey hood, so are fairly easy to distinguish.

SILVER GULL

(Syn.: Hartlaub's gull)

Larus (Chroicocephalus) novaehollandiae

Wing span 33 inches.

This is another gull of the southern hemisphere, though, in the Atlantic sector, it is confined to South Africa.

It is a white gull with a grey mantle, red legs and feet. The adult bird is therefore very similar to,

Kittiwake

BIRDS OF THE ATLANTIC OCEAN

though smaller than, the grey-headed gull whose range it overlaps in South Africa. The head, however, is always pure white both in summer and winter. Immature birds have a mottled brown back and a narrow brown sub-terminal tail bar. Their bills are brown and their legs grey.

The South African race of this species, *hartlaubi*, breeds in western Cape Province, laying its eggs between August and December.

KITTIWAKE

Larus (Rissa) tridactylus

Wing span 39 inches.

The name of this, one of the gentlest and most graceful of all gulls, is onomatopœic. It is a close representation of the bird's call. The kittiwake is also the most pelagic of all gulls, being seldom seen near land except in the breeding season.

A medium sized gull – white with grey mantle – it has dark grey, nearly black legs and a yellow bill. The easiest distinguishing mark, however, is that the black wing tips have no white mirrors. In winter, when the bird may be encountered thousands of miles from land, the adult has a grey smudge on the nape of the neck.

Immature kittiwakes, sometimes known as 'tarrocks', are very striking birds. They have white heads, underparts and tails. Their bills are dark grey like their feet and they have a dull grey mantle. Superimposed on this pattern, however, is a very

1. Silver Gull.   2. Slender-billed Gull.   3. Grey-headed Gull.
4. Laughing Gull (immature).   5. Laughing Gull.
6. Laughing Gull (winter plumage).

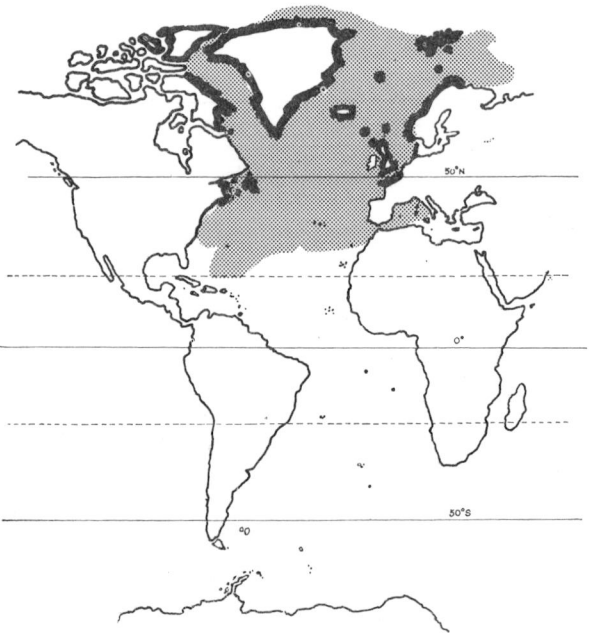

striking W of black – from wing tip to wing crank to rump – a jet black terminal bar to the tail and a black yoke. There is a grey smudge behind the eye.

Kittiwakes nest in large colonies on cliffs throughout the Arctic and temperate North Atlantic oceans. They frequently nest on ledges with auks and guillemots. The nests are placed, usually high on the cliff face, on small, inaccessible ledges. Two eggs are laid any time from April to July. They may be buff, olive or pinkish buff – even pale blue – spotted with brown and blotched with grey. Both sexes share the incubation duties, which may last up to thirty days; both parents also feed and protect the chicks. The chicks will fly at four to six weeks.

In winter, they range over the vast expanse of the ocean from the ice-edge in the north to the Sargasso Sea in the south. There are numerous records of

ringed birds crossing the Atlantic and they are also frequently seen in the Mediterranean.

A kittiwake is unique among gulls in that it can, and frequently does, swim underwater in pursuit of small fish.

are large. Eggs, which are brown marked with darker brown – usually three in number – are laid from April to July, depending on the latitude of the colony.

Out of the breeding season, they wander southward to about latitude 30°S.

LAUGHING GULL

Larus (Atricilla) atricilla

Wing span 42 inches.

This is somewhat similar to the black-headed gull – red bill and feet, white beneath and grey on top – but the hood is black, not chocolate, and the mantle is a far deeper grey than that of the other. Within the black hood, also, there is a small white crescent above and below each eye. The immature bird is more uniformly pale brown on its head; a darker bird altogether than the immature black-headed gull. The adult bird in full breeding plumage has a roseate hue on its white breast feathers. In winter, the black head almost disappears, though there remains a suffused patch of grey behind the eyes and on the nape.

Laughing gulls are birds of the temperate and tropical western Atlantic. They breed from Maine in the north, south through the Caribbean to northern South America. The nest is on the ground, among sand dunes or on marsh land, similarly placed, in fact, to that of the black-headed gull. The colonies

FRANKLIN'S GULL

Larus (Atricilla) pipixcan

Wing span 35 inches.

Smaller than, but very similar to, the laughing gull in appearance, Franklin's gull can be distinguished by the white outer tips to the primaries. It is the only gull which breeds in the north and migrates completely from the vicinity of its breeding sites to tropical waters and the southern hemisphere, in winter. The immature bird differs only from young laughing gulls in that the brown shading is absent from the breast – a difficult difference to spot in the field.

This gull is a lake breeder, large colonies being scattered across Canada, around the Great Lakes and south to Utah. It is also a marsh breeder. Colonies are large and are frequently among quite high reeds. The nest is a large floating mass reminiscent of a grebe's nest. The three eggs are laid in May or June and are pale olive with dark splodges.

In winter, the birds move down to the Gulf coast and, though not in the South Atlantic, down as far as central Chile.

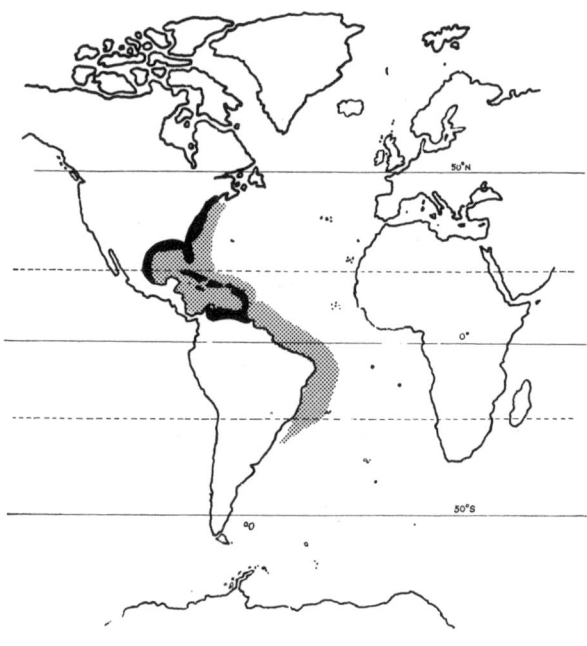

ORDER *LARO-LIMICOLAE*

MEDITERRANEAN GULL

Larus (Atricilla) melanocephalus

Wing span 36 inches.

As the range of this gull overlaps that of the black-headed gull in Europe, confusion between the two species can arise. But, in breeding plumage, the adult bird has a black – not a chocolate – head, and no black tips to the wings. The dark hood comes down to cover the throat as well. It is a smaller bird than the laughing gull, but has the white crescents above and below the eyes. However, no confusion between these two species can arise as they frequent completely different parts of the world. They may well be fairly closely related. In winter, the head is white streaked with black.

Immature birds have a mottled brown head, neck and back, the outer primaries are dark brown, and there is a sub-terminal brown tail bar.

The bird is an inland breeder in south-eastern Europe and Asia Minor, but wanders throughout the Mediterranean and Black Sea in winter. It also winters on the Spanish and Portuguese coasts and around the Bay of Biscay. It has been recorded occasionally as far north as Britain.

Sub-family *Sterninae* – terns and noddies

Although obviously related to gulls, terns have many marked differences both in appearance and habit. They are dainty creatures with a graceful, rather bouncy flight. They are fish eaters and do not normally eat refuse. They are quarrelsome and argumentative, and not averse to a bit of stealing here and there, but they are not wholesale murderers as so many gulls are.

All terns have forked tails; many of them have greatly elongated outer tail feathers. They have been aptly nicknamed sea swallows.

Terns are birds of warmer, gentler climes than gulls. Many reside in the tropics and the warmer temperate zones and those that do penetrate the polar regions of the globe do so only in summer and then migrate great distances to warmer winter quarters.

Terns are short-legged in comparison with gulls. Their feet are webbed, but they seldom swim. They fish by diving, sometimes from considerable heights, catching their prey a few inches below the surface.

Both sexes are alike in all species of tern. The birds are nearly all colonial nesters, with only a few exceptions, laying their eggs in a shallow hollow in the ground.

Many terns are river and fresh water birds; all those here could be seen at sea.

LARGE-BILLED TERN

Sterna (Phaetusa) simplex

Wing span 36 inches.

Strangely enough, the first bird in order in the sub-family has a nearly square tail. It is a river tern, but does wander across the sea and, of course, may be seen fishing in and off river estuaries.

It is a white bird with a black cap and grey mantle. The wing tips are dark brown; the legs olive green except for the webs of the feet which are yellow. Young birds are mottled grey and brown above and white beneath.

This tern breeds on sandbanks in the large rivers of South America, where two pale eggs speckled and blotched with grey or brown are laid in September or October. The young, when hatched, are downy, vaguely speckled and very well camouflaged as, indeed, are nearly all the eggs and young of terns.

Out of the breeding season it may be seen on the eastern coast of South America and possibly as far away from the mainland as Cuba.

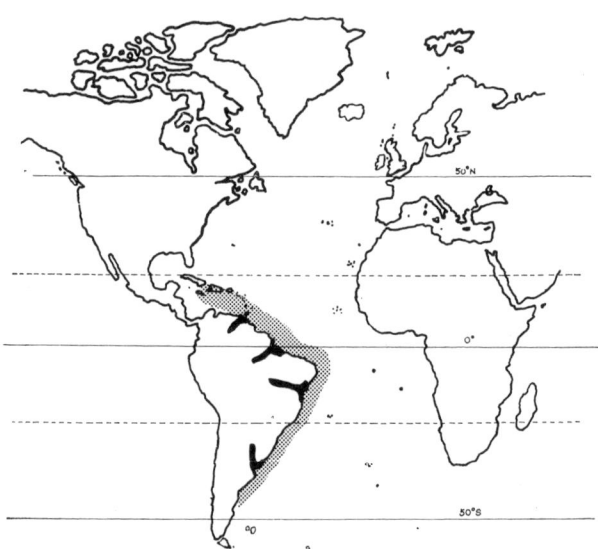

Little Tern

LITTLE TERN

(Syn.: least tern)

Sterna (Sternula) albifrons

Wing span 20 inches.

Anywhere along the coast of western Europe or the eastern United States on a bright summer's day when the sea is still and the haze is a hot white veil, you may hear repeated, shrill and grating cries coming apparently from nowhere. Look very carefully, quite close above you, and they will suddenly appear; delicate bounding, wraith-like birds with white foreheads, black caps and long, streamer, swallow-tails. These are little terns. Their size is diagnostic, as also is the white forehead which gives them their specific name. Their bills and legs are yellow.

Common throughout the world, little terns which breed in tropical waters are fairly static, while those which breed in the British Isles, northern Europe and the Baltic move south in winter to warmer parts.

They do not usually elect to breed in colonies of any size. Just one or two nests may be found on a stretch of sandy beach, a harbour bar or any flat which may even be covered at highest spring tides. The eggs, small and pointed, pale buff with brown blotches, are so well camouflaged that many escape the notice of even the sharpest-eyed predators. Individual birds, moreover, do not seem to be tied to the same nesting site each year.

The birds of the western Atlantic – the east coast of the United States, Bermuda, the Bahamas and the Caribbean – are known as least terns and are of a race which is specified *Sterna albifrons antillarum*.

The little tern's feeding habits are typical of a great number of its family. Flying around with its rather bouncy, slow and deliberate wing beat, with its head dipped so that the bill is pointed vertically down at right angles to the line of flight, it will suddenly hesitate, swing sharply round, hover a moment and then dive with closed wings, head first into the water. Immersion is only momentary, and the bird bobs to the surface almost at once, spreads its wings upwards and is off into the air, more often than not with a wriggling, silver fish hanging from its bill. The bird will swallow the fish at leisure and may possibly shake itself free of a fine spray of water drops before starting all over again. This process is accompanied by a shrill call which can best be described as a metallic creak.

BLACK TERN

Sterna nigra

Wing span 21 inches.

The black tern is essentially a bird of inland marshes, ponds and lakes in the breeding season. It has a shortish, forked, grey tail and short, broad wings which are grey on top, slightly lighter beneath. The head and forepart of the body are completely black in the breeding season, but, out of it, the body is pale, only the hood remaining black. Immature birds are mottled brown on the back and hood, but already have their grey wings.

The black tern breeds over most northern land masses – as far south as Pennsylvania in the American continent and as far south as Spain in Europe. The

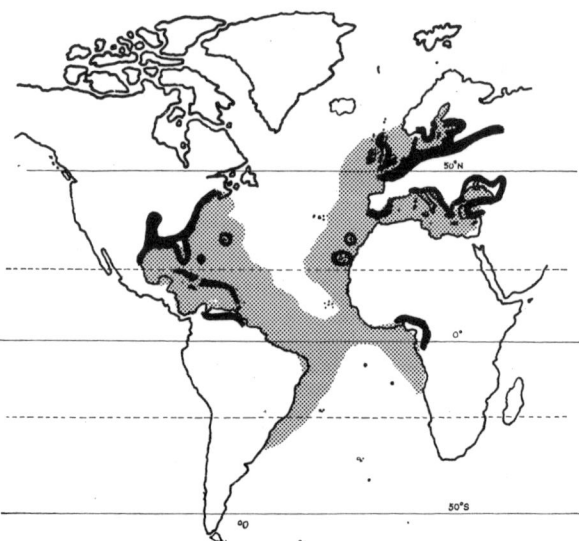

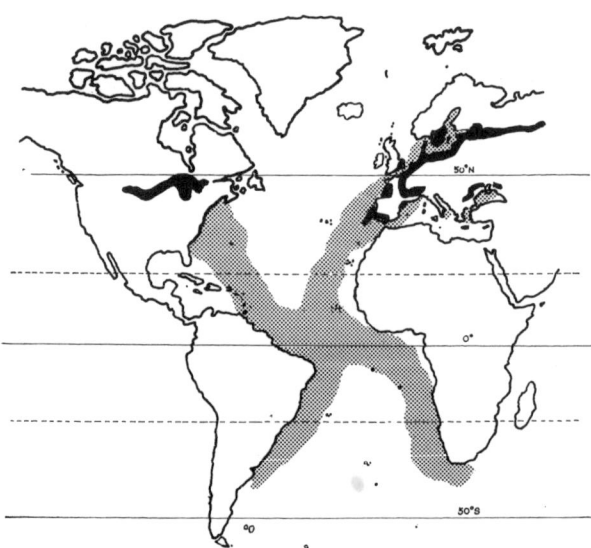

ORDER *LARO-LIMICOLAE*

nest is usually placed on floating vegetation in marshes or lakes and is a simple grass cup in which three heavily brown-blotched, olive eggs are laid in May, June or July.

In the northern autumn, migrating black terns make direct for the nearest coast and thence move south to their winter quarters along the coastal waters of northern South America and South Africa. When at sea, in 'winter', they feed on small fish and surface marine life. They seldom dive like other terns, preferring to pluck their food from the surface.

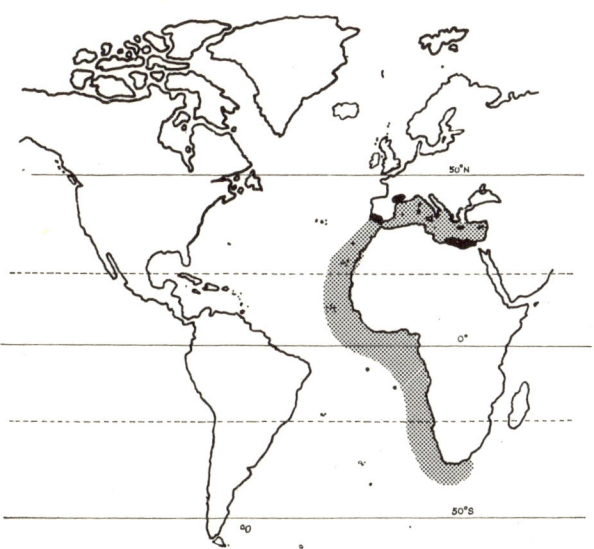

WHITE-WINGED BLACK TERN

Sterna leucoptera

Wing span 22 inches.

Like the black tern, this is a fresh water bird which rarely flies over the sea except at migration time. It is, however, far less common and is confined to the eastern side of the Atlantic. Very similar in shape and size to the black tern, its head, neck and upper back are black in summer though mottled with white in the winter. Some of the wing coverts and the edges of the wing are white. The underparts are black in summer and white in winter. Under the tail is white. The bill is red in summer and black in winter. The feet are a deep orange. Immature birds are like the adults in winter plumage but paler.

This species breeds in central and southern Europe and migrates south to Africa. Stragglers have been recorded in the British Isles and, rarely, as far west as the United States and the West Indies.

WHISKERED TERN

Sterna hybrida

Wing span 30 inches.

In summer, this is a generally grey bird with a black cap, but with a conspicuous white streak running back on the sides of the head from the red bill to the nape of the neck. The abdomen is very deep grey, almost black. In winter the underparts are white. Immature birds are like adults in winter plumage, but the crown is brownish and the mantle mottled.

It is another fresh water breeding tern, resident in southern Europe and North Africa. When not breeding, the movement is mostly south to South Africa, but it has been recorded in Germany, the British Isles and even in Barbados.

SOOTY TERN

(Syn.: wideawake)

Sterna fuscata

Wing span 32 inches.

This is unique among terns in its clear definition; very dark above and white beneath. The cap is black, but the face is white. A conspicuous line runs from the middle of the cap, through the eye forward to the black bill. Except for the grey undersides of the primaries, the bird is snow white beneath. The legs are black and the tail is deeply forked, dark above and dusky white beneath. Immature birds are mottled brown on their backs, have a sooty head and

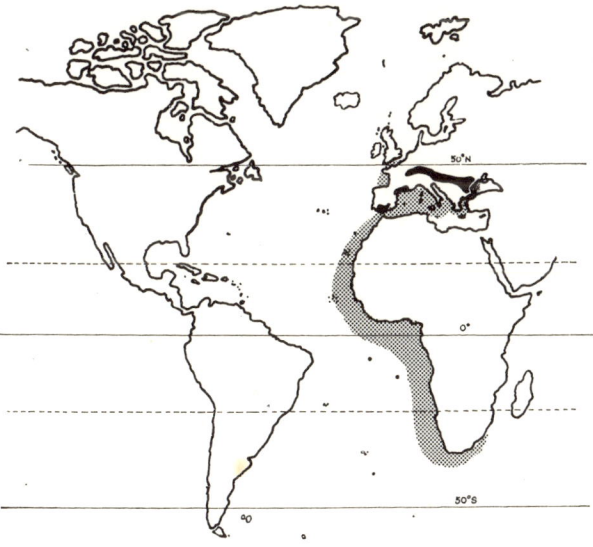

127

BIRDS OF THE ATLANTIC OCEAN

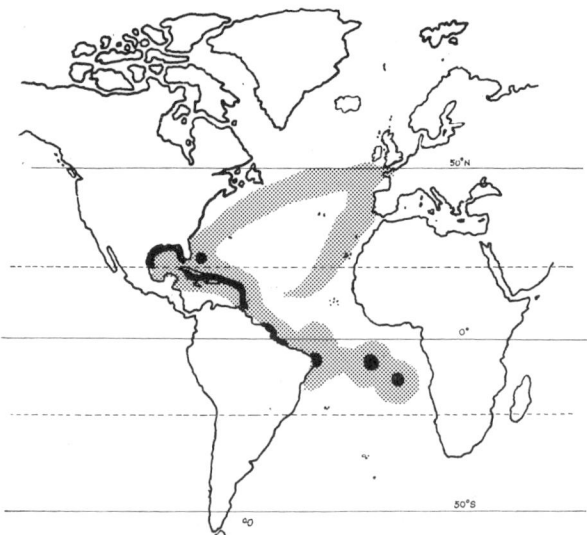

1. Damara Tern. 2. Sooty Tern.
3. Whiskered Tern (summer plumage).
4. Whiskered Tern (winter plumage). 5. Large-billed Tern.
6. Black Tern (summer plumage).
7. Black Tern (winter plumage). 8. Bridled Tern.
9. White-winged Black Tern (summer plumage).
10. White-winged Black Tern (winter plumage).

chest, and 'pale off' towards the abdomen and under the tail. The tail is forked, but not as truly 'swallow-tail' as the adult bird.

Sooty terns breed in immense colonies through tropical and sub-tropical seas. There they scream day and night, hence the name 'wideawake'. Colonies occur on islands and coasts on both sides of the North Atlantic. One egg is laid on flat ground, on rocks or even on cliff ledges. It is almost white, with reddish brown spots. There is no fixed breeding period.

Considering the enormous numbers of breeding birds sooty terns are seldom seen in any numbers outside the breeding season. They are, however, wholly pelagic when not at the nesting sites and have been recorded as far north as Nova Scotia and the British Isles.

The sooty tern, like the frigate bird, never gets wet when feeding. Its feathers are not water-proofed, so it neither dives nor settles on the water, but snatches fish from the surface while airborne.

BRIDLED TERN

(Syn.: brown-winged tern)

Sterna anaetheta

Wing span 30 inches.

The pattern of this tern is similar to that of sooty terns, but only the cap is black. The topsides of the wings are brown and the back and central feathers of the tail are grey. The white face-patch is rather narrower than that of the sooty tern and the bill is thinner. Immature birds are mottled brown above and dirty white beneath. In both adult and immature birds, the whitish colour across the neck – the division between the head cap and the back – is distinctive.

Bridled terns breed in colonies, often alongside sooty terns and other sea birds. The single white

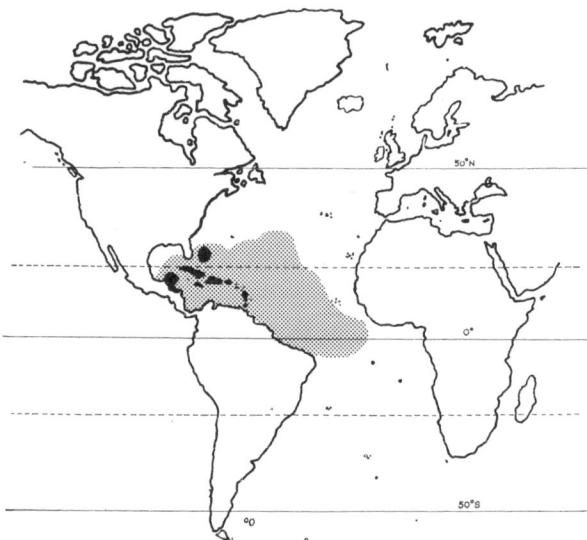

egg, spotted with brown, is laid well hidden among rocks and crannies. In the Atlantic, colonies occur in the Bahamas and the West Indies, but the bird is found in tropical and sub-tropical seas throughout the world. When not breeding, it is strictly oceanic.

DAMARA TERN

Sterna balaenarum

Wing span 19 inches.

This tiny tern is the smallest of all – even smaller than the little tern, from which it can be instantly distinguished when in breeding plumage, by its black forehead and slender black bill. A white bird, with typical tern swallow-tail and grey back, it has a slight greying of the breast which is also diagnostic. In winter, adult birds have some white mottling of the face and crown, but the black bill is still distinct. Immature birds are slightly darker on top than adults.

Restricted to the south-west coast of Africa, it ranges from the Congo coast to the Cape and breeds throughout its range. Eggs can be laid at any time of year dependent on latitude.

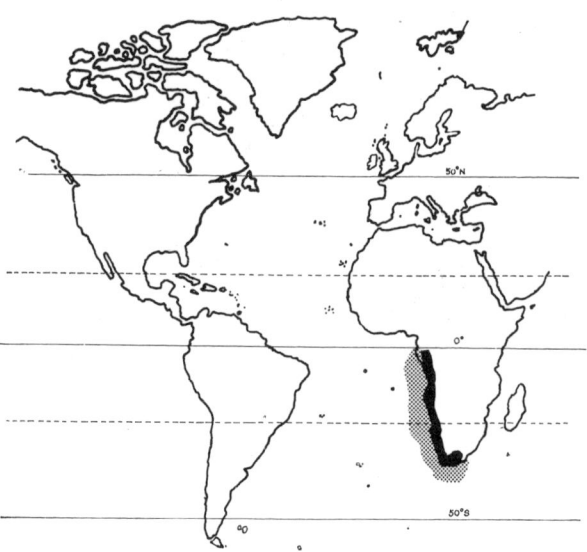

TRUDEAU'S TERN

Sterna trudeaui

Wing span 30 inches.

Trudeau's tern is a bird of temperate South America. On the Atlantic coast it may be seen from Rio south to northern Patagonia. Unlike most terns, its

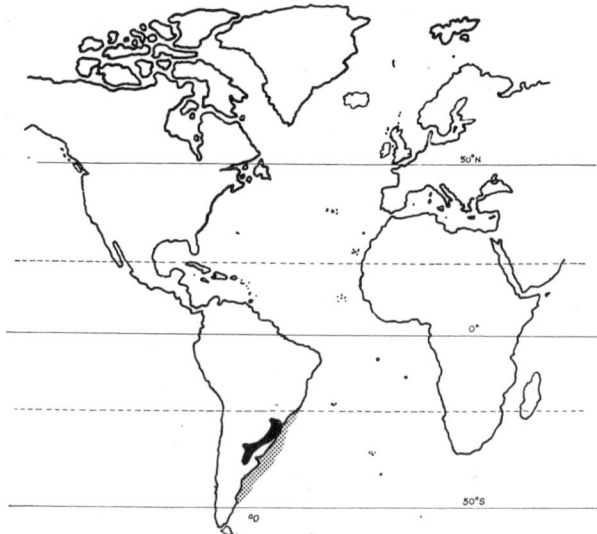

head is white with only a black patch in front of the eye and a black streak behind it. The upper parts of the wings are pearl grey, darker at the tips. The tail and rump are almost white; the breast and belly grey. It has orange legs and feet and a yellow bill with a black band. Immature birds have a greyish crown and the mantle is mottled with brown.

Trudeau's tern is an inland breeder in the Argentine where its nesting season is from October to February.

FORSTER'S TERN

Sterna forsteri

Wing span 30 inches.

In breeding plumage, the adult Forster's tern resembles the common tern, though it is slightly larger. Its longer tail and orange and black bill are also distinctive. However, it is mostly an inland breeder and is therefore more likely to be seen at sea in winter plumage, in which garb it closely resembles Trudeau's tern – a greyish white head with a black streak running through the eye, grey mantle, white rump and underparts. The bill, however, is rather stout and dull orange and black.

Forster's tern flies with a more staccato wing beat than the common tern. It is also an insect eater as well as a fisherman. The bird's call, too, is distinctive. Apart from a high *'click click'* – more associated with tropic birds than terns – there is a soft, low pitched wheeze which is not at all tern-like.

Not as colonial as some terns, it often lays its three olive-brown eggs – spotted and lined with brown – on

Roseate Tern

BIRDS OF THE ATLANTIC OCEAN

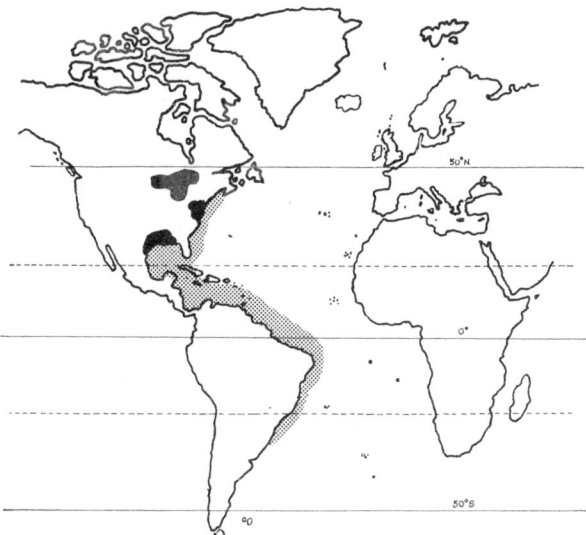

small rafts of rotting vegetation which have collected and drifted to the shore. Sometimes the eggs are laid in marshes or on bare, sandy, shell-strewn ground. Breeding mostly takes place on inland lakes in Canada and the United States, though some do stay on the coast, breeding from Washington, round the Florida coast to Texas.

In winter, when the birds are easily distinguished from common terns, they range south to the Gulf and northern South American coasts, sometimes as far as Brazil. It is here that they could easily be confused with Trudeau's tern, although, of course, the breeding season of the one coincides with the winter wandering season of the other.

1. Forster's Tern (summer plumage).
2. Forster's Tern (winter plumage).   3. Trudeau's Tern.
4. Common Tern (summer plumage).
5. Common Tern (winter plumage).
6. Arctic Tern (summer plumage).
7. Arctic Tern (summer plumage).   8. Arctic Tern (immature).
9. Arctic Tern (winter plumage).   10. Arctic Tern (immature).
11. Antarctic Tern.
12. South American Tern and Antarctic Tern (immature).
13. South American Tern.   14. Sandwich Tern (summer plumage).
15. Sandwich Tern (winter plumage).

ARCTIC TERN

Sterna paradisaea

Wing span 30 inches.

Large numbers of these beautiful, aggressive little birds spend all but about two months of the year in permanent daylight. For, apart from a fantastic journey from Arctic circle to Antarctic circle and back, they live in the two regions of midnight sun. Not all of them do this, but the usual pattern of migration is that birds which live farthest north go farthest south and those which do not go so far one way do not go so far the other either. In any case, whether they actually make the whole distance or not, Arctic terns are probably the world's record holders for long distance migration; a round trip of anything up to 22,000 miles.

They are ash-grey underneath, have a black cap, a blood-red bill with, sometimes, a small dark area

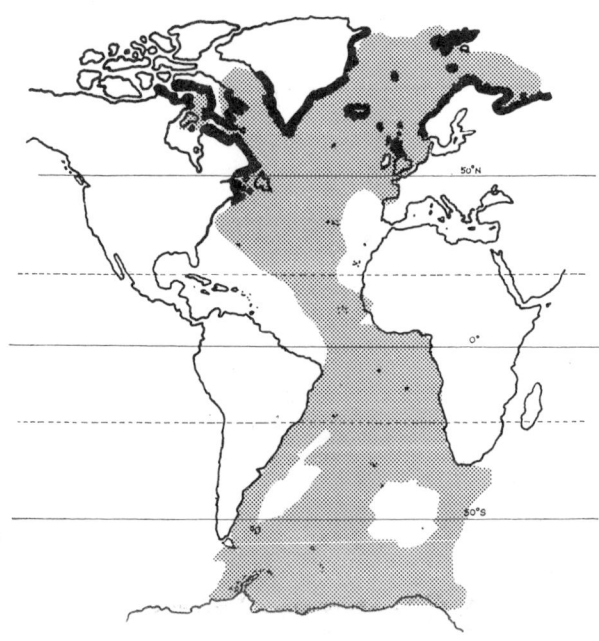

at the tip and very short, coral-red legs and feet. The tail streamers are very long in adult breeding plumage. The cap is jet black, coming well back to a point on the nape of the neck. The mantle is pearl grey. Immature birds have a yellow bill with a black tip and yellow feet. Their backs are slightly mottled with brown. In winter, the bills of old and young become black; the legs and feet nearly all black.

Arctic terns breed, sometimes in large colonies, sometimes in small scattered groups, all round Arctic shores as far south as north Britain in the east and Maine in the west. Two eggs, which vary from dark brown with darker blotches to quite pale buff with brown and black markings, are placed on the ground, on sand, on grass or in swampy places.

Approaching a large colony is an exciting and sometimes painful experience. Birds defend their nests with incredible ferocity for such small creatures. With a blood-curdling scream, something like *'kee-aarm'*, with accent on the second syllable and a threatening rolling of the 'r', they dive straight at one's face, sometimes even striking and drawing blood. It is an interesting fact that instinct seems to direct their attack to the highest point of the intruder. Thus, if a pole or fishing rod is carried, attacks are directed at its tip – a useful thing to know when paying a social call on Arctic terns!

As soon as breeding is finished in August or September, they move off across the ocean or travel the length of the Atlantic to take up winter residence in the southern summer in Chile, Patagonia, the islands of the Antarctic, Antarctica itself and South Africa. There is considerable evidence that birds which breed on the Maine coast, the southernmost breeding area of the species, cross the Atlantic to winter in South Africa, its northernmost wintering area.

1. Caspian Tern (winter plumage).
2. Caspian Tern (summer plumage).
3. Royal Tern (winter plumage).
4. Lesser Crested Tern (winter plumage).
5. Royal Tern (summer plumage). 6. White Tern.
7. Lesser Crested Tern (summer plumage).
8. Gull-billed Tern (summer plumage).
9. Gull-billed Tern (winter plumage).
10. Gull-billed Tern (immature). 11. Common Noddy.
12. African Skimmer. 13. White-capped Noddy.

ANTARCTIC TERN

(Syn.: swallow-tailed tern)

Sterna vittata

Wing span 30 inches.

This tern, in breeding plumage, is so similar to the Arctic tern that, if their breeding areas were to overlap, it would be impossible to distinguish them on the wing. However, the Antarctic tern is in breeding plumage when the Arctic tern is in its area displaying its winter plumage of black bill and feet.

In breeding plumage, therefore, the adult of this

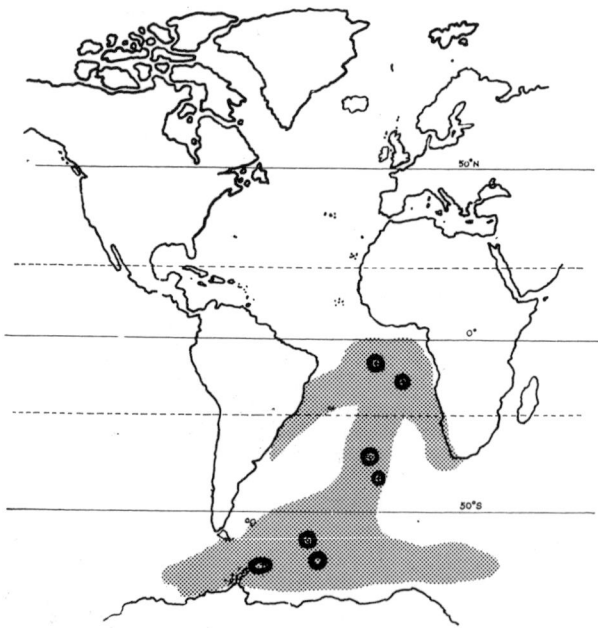

species is pale, smoky-grey beneath, has a black cap, pearl-grey mantle, red bill and orange legs. In winter, the legs and bill are yellow. Immature birds are palely barred on their backs, are white beneath and have dull red legs, bill and feet.

The species is circum-polar in range, breeding on south Atlantic islands from St Helena south to the South Orkneys. Eggs are laid from November to January and, when not breeding, the bird may be seen anywhere in the south Atlantic.

SOUTH AMERICAN TERN

Sterna hirundinacea

Wing span 32 inches

This is another of four, very similar and surely related species. The bird is grey beneath in breeding plumage; white in winter. The cap is black in summer; white, marked with grey and black, in winter. The bill and feet are bright red. It is noticeably larger than the Arctic tern. Again, however, if it were not for the fact that breeding seasons are at opposite ends of the calendar, differentiation would be nearly impossible.

This, as the name implies, is a bird of the South American coast and adjacent sub-Antarctic islands, breeding as far north as Rio. It is no great migrant and will only be seen in the south-western limits of the Atlantic.

COMMON TERN

Sterna hirundo

Wing span 31 inches.

Of slightly more temperature range, the common tern is similar to, though larger than, the Arctic tern. The main differences are that the legs are slightly longer, the underside is white with only a slightly violet hue on the breast and the bill is black from the tip back about a third of the way, before the red portion is reached. The 'swallow-tail' is not as long as that of the Arctic tern. The cry of anger when disturbed is slightly different, the accent being on the first syllable of *'kee-ar'*. Common terns are not quite as reckless in defence of their nests as their northern close relations.

The species breeds around the world in the whole of the temperate zone of the northern hemisphere. In the Atlantic they breed from northern Scandinavia to the Canaries and throughout the Mediterranean in the east, and from Labrador to the Gulf, including Bermuda, the Bahamas and some of the West Indies, in the west. The eggs, which are pale brown or buff with dark blotches, are laid from May to July depending on latitude. Nests are in colonies or single, sometimes in company with other sea birds, and are on the ground.

In winter, birds disperse southward over the ocean, as far south, sometimes, as Cape Horn.

The common tern is the most likely member of the family to be seen in the European and American

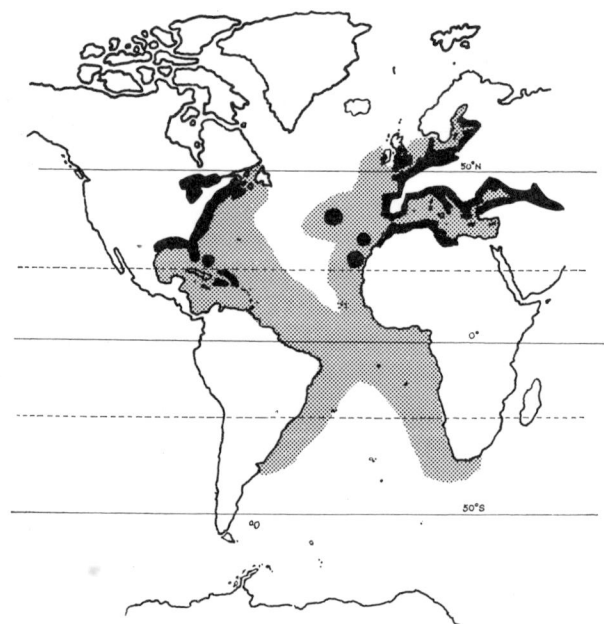

harbours and creeks frequented by man. At sea, they are to be seen everywhere when small fish are driven to the surface by larger ones. Their presence can be a very good pointer to the position of shoals of mackerel and other fish.

ROSEATE TERN

Sterna dougallii

Wing span 30 inches.

This is a long-billed, extremely long-tailed, very slender, very beautiful little tern. At a distance, it could be confused with either the common tern or the Arctic tern, but it is a paler bird, white beneath except for a not very obvious rosy tint. The bill is black with only the very base of it turning orange-red in the breeding season. In winter, adult birds have a white forehead and entirely black bills. Immature birds have a speckled back, browny mottled cap and white forehead. Their legs are a pale orange.

Their alarm note is distinctive, being a hard, harsh *'aark'*, described as like tearing cloth.

Roseate terns are entirely maritime birds, never nesting near fresh water as many others do. They nest in colonies among rocks, on small beaches or sea swards, often in association with other terns and gulls. Two rather pale, sometimes white, lined, speckled or blotched eggs are laid in widely scattered coastal or island sites on both sides of the Atlantic. Egg dates are April to August in the North Atlantic and at any time in the tropics.

When not breeding the bird is entirely maritime – often pelagic – and may be seen from Maine and Scotland down to Brazil and the Cape of Good Hope and throughout the Mediterranean.

SANDWICH TERN

(Syns: elegant tern, Cayenne tern)

Sterna (Thalasseus) sandvicensis

Wing span 33 inches.

Coming into harbour, you may see sitting on a buoy, one or two very smart terns with heavy, crested black caps, pearl-grey backs, black bills with yellow tips, black legs and the purest of pure white undersides. They are, without a doubt, Sandwich terns. Outside the breeding season, the crests disappear and the birds have white face-patches. The young are speckled over the grey of their backs. These largish, strong-flying terns have increased in numbers in recent years and spread north.

The North Atlantic race, *sandvicensis*, breeds on both sides of the Atlantic. In the west, there are colonies from Virginia south to the West Indies; in Europe they breed in north Britain and Denmark, around the straits of Gibraltar and in the central Mediterranean. The South Atlantic race, *eurygnatha*, breeds on the coasts of Venezuela and Brazil, and a Pacific race, *elegans*, may sometimes wander to the coasts of the Gulf of Mexico. The eggs are large and vary in colour from reddy-brown, with dark streaks and splodges, to pure white with just a few black spots.

Out of the breeding season, Sandwich terns have been recorded the whole way down both sides of the Atlantic.

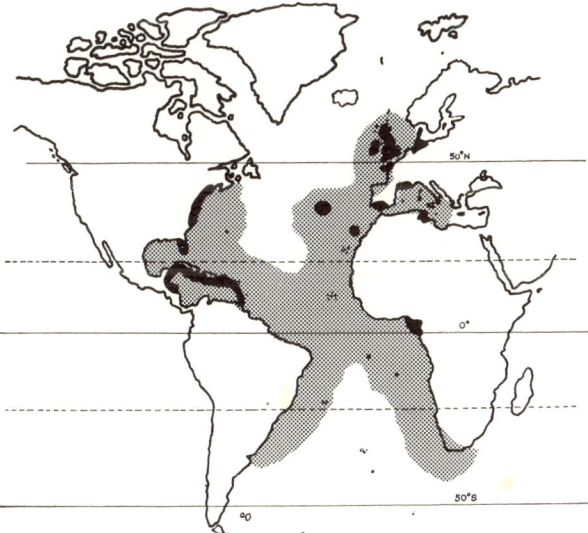
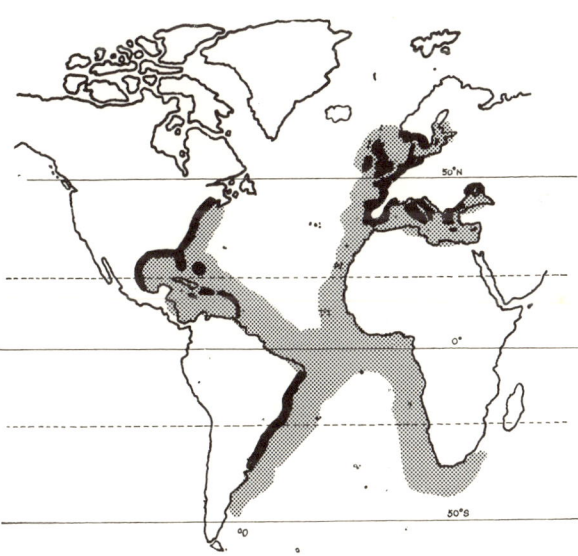

BIRDS OF THE ATLANTIC OCEAN

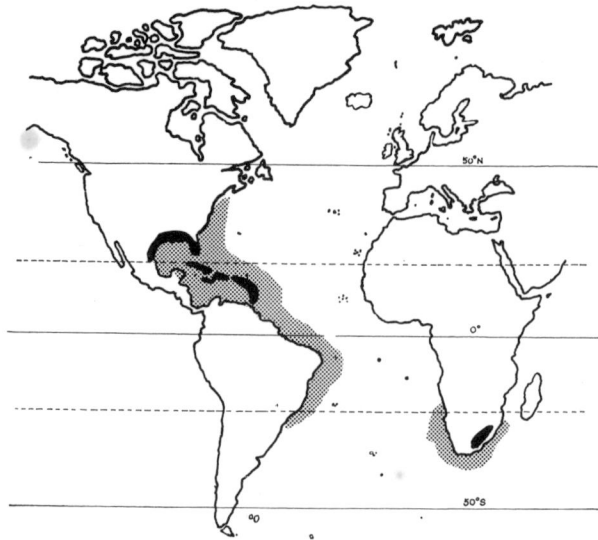

LESSER CRESTED TERN

Sterna (Thalasseus) bengalensis

Wing span 33 inches.

This Mediterranean tern could be confused with the Sandwich tern, though the bill is yellow-orange, not black. The crest is much more noticeable and is not simply a feature of breeding plumage. In winter plumage – and this is the important one in relation to the areas covered by this work – the crown cap and crest are streaked with white. Immature birds have an almost white crown.

The lesser crested tern breeds on the coasts of the Red Sea and east Africa, so it is not an Atlantic breeding bird. In winter, however, it spreads to the eastern Mediterranean.

ROYAL TERN

(Syn.: crested tern)

Sterna (Thalasseus) maxima

Wing span 43 inches.

The crown and nape of this very large tern are black with elongated feathers. Sometimes the forehead also is black, but usually white or streaked white. In winter the whole crown is streaked with white. The mantle is pale grey and the deeply forked tail is greyish-white. Underneath it is white and the feet are black and the bill heavy orange. The young have almost white heads, striated brown backs, and yellow bills and feet.

Royal terns nest throughout the West Indies and on southern coasts of the United States. They lay their two eggs, which are white or buff, spotted with dark brown, in a hollow scraped in the open sand. Egg dates are April to June and colonies are usually large and crowded.

They are common all around the Caribbean and, in winter, spread as far north as New Jersey and as far south as the Argentine.

Another race, *bergii*, spreads into the South Atlantic from the Cape of Good Hope as far north as Walfish Bay. It is a South African breeder at the extreme western limit of its breeding range.

CASPIAN TERN

Sterna (Thalasseus) caspia

Wing span 53 inches.

If for no other reason, the Caspian tern is readily recognisable by its large size. It is a large bird by any standards, being almost as big as a herring gull. The jet-black cap, the forked tail and its tern-like flight and habit of plunging for fish immediately identify it as a tern. It is a white bird with a pale grey mantle and a large, brilliant red bill. The feet and legs are black and the primaries dark grey – almost black – on the underside. In winter the head-cap is streaked with white and immature birds have brown mottling on their backs.

Caspian terns breed in scattered colonies or singly on the coasts of Europe, Africa and North America. They wander considerable distances in the winter and may be seen anywhere from north Britain to South Africa or from Labrador to Mexico. Two or three eggs are laid on sandy or rocky ground

Black Skimmer

BIRDS OF THE ATLANTIC OCEAN

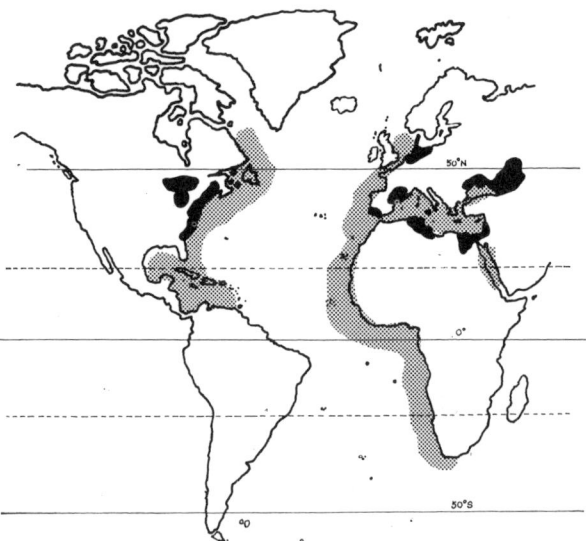

or on floating vegetation near the shores of shallow lakes. They are light buff, lightly spotted with dark brown and appear at any time of the year.

GULL-BILLED TERN

Sterna (Gelochelidon) nilotica

Wing span 34 inches.

The short, fat, gull-like bill instantly distinguishes this tern. In fact, apart from its noticeably forked tail, it might be a small gull. But look at the flight! The bouncy, tern beat and method of progression, and the downward held bill, stamp it as a tern. It is a very pale bird, white beneath and very pale grey above. Its bill and feet are black and, of course, in summer the adult bird has a black cap. In winter, the head is nearly white, only vaguely marked with grey and black. Immature birds are like winter adults, but have rather yellowy legs and the suggestion of pale brown marking on their backs.

The bird's distribution is world wide, although it has become rare in the Atlantic. In the west it breeds from New Jersey south to Brazil; in the east in the Baltic, in Denmark and some Mediterranean and Black Sea coasts. It also breeds inland. The three creamy buff eggs with a few brown spots are normally laid from April to June, usually in depression on shell-strewn shores.

COMMON NODDY

(Syns: noddy tern, brown noddy)
Anoüs stolidus

Wing span 32 inches.

Birds of the tern family which are strictly confined to the warm water areas of the world are called noddies; presumably because of their greeting habits. A considerable amount of bowing and nodding goes on in the large island colonies in which they breed. Two species are concerned in the Atlantic area.

The common noddy is a brown bird with a rounded tail. It is entirely brown, with slightly darker wing tips, except for a white cap which, in the adult bird, extends back to the nape of the neck and, in the immature bird, does not go further back than the centre of the crown.

It breeds all round the Caribbean and in tropical

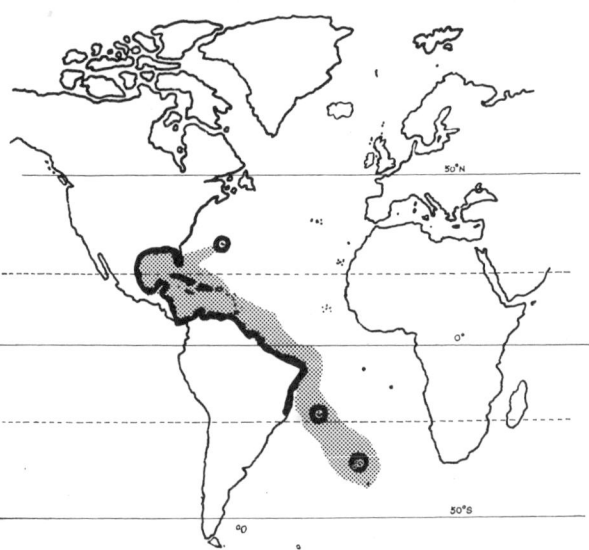

ORDER *LARO-LIMICOLAE*

South America. It has even been known to breed as far north as Bermuda and as far south as Tristan da Cunha. A single egg is laid on rocks or ledges, in nests of sticks and seaweed, on grass clumps, in shrubs or even in trees. The eggs are buff, lightly spotted with brown, and are laid throughout the year.

Though noddies are confined to the western Atlantic, they have world wide distribution in other tropical oceans.

WHITE-CAPPED NODDY

(Syn.: lesser noddy)

Anoüs tenuirostris

Wing span 21 inches.

This is a much smaller bird than the common noddy; its plumage is darker and the white cap whiter, making a greater overall contrast. It is a tree breeder, sometimes nesting at considerable heights. The breeding range extends from Honduras, south-east through the Caribbean and along the north coast of South America to Tristan da Cunha.

Noddies are not diving birds. They prefer to hover and pluck their prey from the surface of the sea. They drink and bathe without alighting and, although they are perfectly capable of swimming, prefer to perch on a rock or a stump. Both common and white-capped noddies remain within tropical waters, mostly within fairly close distance of their nesting sites even when not breeding. As with the common noddy, the white-capped noddy may lay eggs at any time of the year.

Another race of the species, *minutus,* is found in the Indian Ocean.

WHITE TERN

(Syn.: love tern)

Anoüs (Gygis) albus

Wing span 31 inches.

This is the only pure white tern, the only colour occuring in the whole pattern of the bird being a marked black ring round the eye and dark bill and legs. Like some other tropical birds, the colours of the bill and the legs vary considerably within the species; the legs even varying from black to pale blue. Immature birds have a black spot behind the eye instead of the complete eye ring and a few black shafts appear on the wing tips and tail. Its tail is very long and deeply forked and as it has a particular penchant for trees, the white tern can hardly be confused with any other species which occurs in the Atlantic.

The white tern is a bird of exclusively tropical range. In the Atlantic it nests off the bulge of Brazil, on South Trinidad and Ascension Islands. A single pale egg is laid from May to January, on a rock or, more often, on a high branch of a tree.

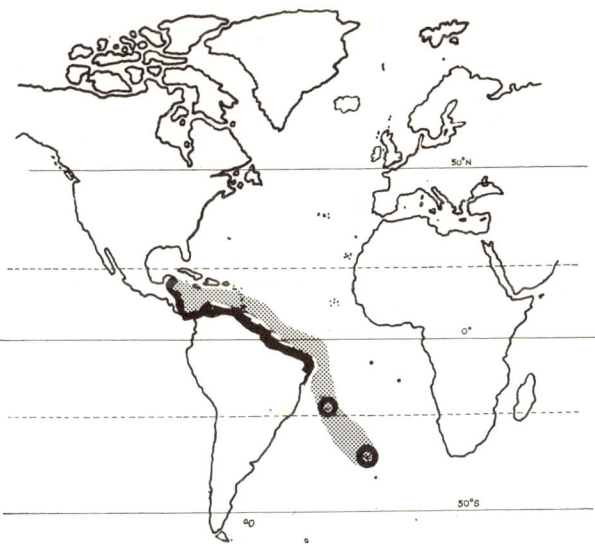

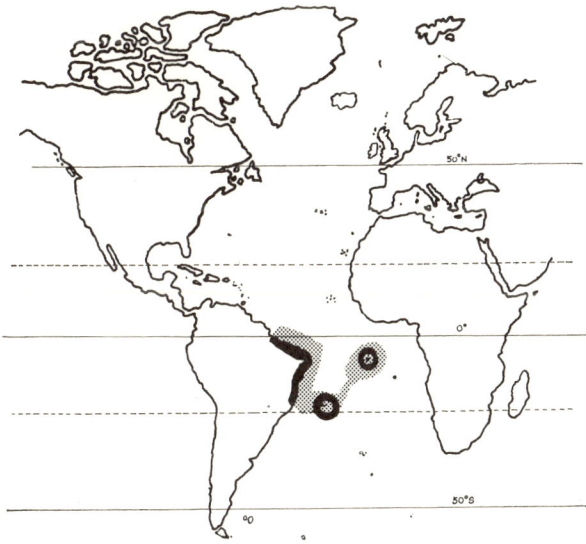

FAMILY *RYNCHOPIDAE* – SKIMMERS

Skimmers or scissor-bills, as they are sometimes called, are strange birds which, if it wasn't for the grotesque adaptation of their bills, might easily be thought to be large terns. The lower mandible, however, is extended well beyond the upper. Both its edges are squeezed together to form a knife edge which, when the bill is closed, fits neatly into a groove-like recess in the upper mandible.

The real use of this curious shaped bill is not completely understood. The bird flies low over the water with the lower mandible extended so that the tip ploughs the surface of the water. It was thought that marine animal and vegetable food was thus scooped up into the bird's mouth after the fashion of an express steam locomotive picking up water on the move. Latterly, however, a theory has been put forward that the scooping of the surface of the water is not, in itself, a method of feeding, but rather a method of luring small fish to the surface to be picked up on the return run.

Whichever theory is right, feeding on the wing is certainly not the only method. Skimmers stand around on sandbanks most of the day, snapping up food from the water's edge, as opportunity occurs. Feeding on the wing takes place either in the early morning, late evening or by moonlight.

Skimmers are essentially birds of large river estuaries and bays. They spend most of their lives in the vicinity of sandbanks. They lay three to five eggs in a scoop in the sand. The young, for protection, rely entirely on their camouflaged down and their ability to stay absolutely still when danger is imminent.

Immature skimmers have rather shorter lower mandibles than adults. Chicks and

1. Razorbill (winter plumage). 2. Razorbill (immature).
3. Razorbill (summer plumage). 4. Guillemot (winter plumage).
5. Guillemot (bridled form). 6. Guillemot.
7. Arctic Guillemot (summer plumage).
8. Arctic Guillemot (winter plumage).
9. Black Guillemot (winter plumage).
10. Dovekie (winter plumage).
11. Black Guillemot (summer plumage).
12. Dovekie (summer plumage).
13. Puffin (winter plumage). 14. Puffin (summer plumage).
15. Puffin (immature). 16. Razorbill.

fledglings have normal bills with which they can pick up food in the ordinary fashion, but as soon as the proper plumage comes in, the lower mandibles grow forward with remarkable rapidity. The noise which large congregations of skimmers make has been likened to the sound of a pack of hounds in full cry.

BLACK SKIMMER

Rynchops nigra

Wing span 46 inches.

The curious bill with its grossly elongated lower mandible – red with a black tip – instantly distinguishes the skimmer. The wings are very long in relation to the size of the bird.

The black skimmer – the American, Atlantic skimmer – has a black crown, a black back and mantle, and a forked tail. There is a narrow white dividing line between the black of the crown and the black of the back, and the forehead is white. The underparts, including the undersides of the wings and tail, are white. The legs and feet are orange. Immature birds have a shorter lower mandible. The upper parts are brown, streaked with white or grey and the underparts are mottled. The bill and feet are brown.

Black skimmers breed on the eastern coast of the United States, of Brazil, Uraguay and the Argentine, mostly in the estuaries of large rivers. In recent years, man and his predatory camp followers – cats, dogs, rats, etc. – have driven skimmer colonies from most of the solid islands in these areas. So the birds have tended more and more to nest on low sand spits which are only just clear of, but everlastingly threatened by, high tides.

The three to five pale blue to buff eggs, heavily spotted with brown, are laid in the spring of either hemisphere. The young, when first hatched, are round, highly camouflaged, downy balls.

AFRICAN SKIMMER

Rynchops flavirostris

Wing span 41 inches.

This is the skimmer of the African rivers and coasts. It is similar to, but smaller than, the black skimmer, and the undersides, instead of being white, are brown. The lower and longer mandible of the bill is yellow instead of orange. The upper mandible is bright red. The bill of young birds is yellow with a black tip. There can, however, be no confusion between the two species as their habitats are separated by the Atlantic Ocean.

African skimmers breed on large rivers and estuaries from Dakar to the Cape of Good Hope. They also nest in the Red Sea and on the upper reaches of the Nile. Three to five buff to blue, spotted eggs are laid in colonies on open sandbanks. Out of the breeding season, birds may be seen anywhere in the vicinity of their breeding grounds. Some, also, come down the Nile to Egypt and the Suez Canal area.

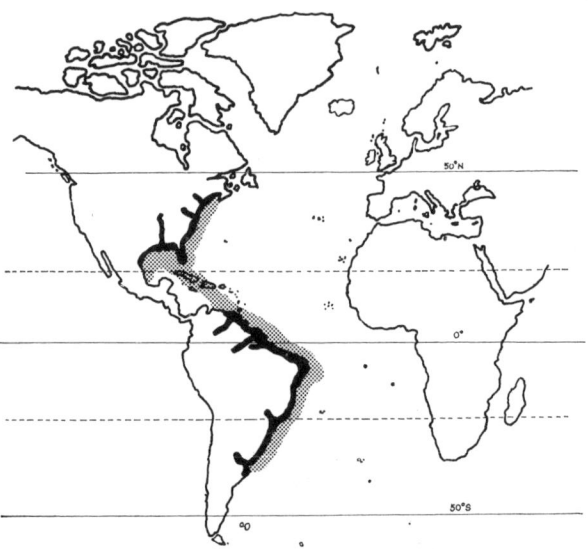
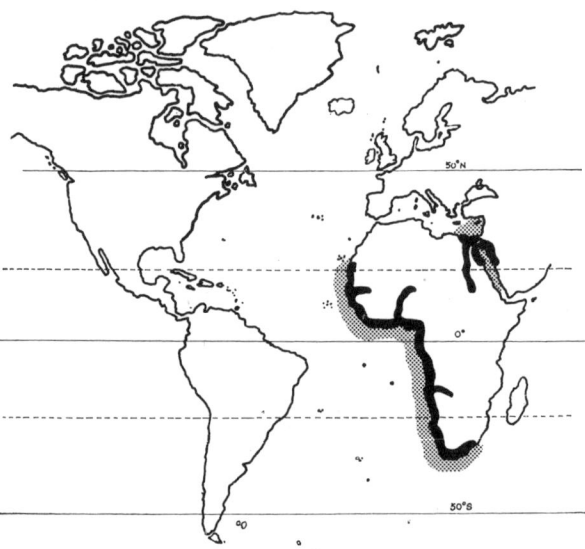

FAMILY *ALCIDAE* – AUKS

Written into the history of this, the last family of ocean birds, is the everlasting and shameful indictment of man – the story of the tragic and inexcusable extermination of the great auk.

Until the middle of the seventeenth century, the great auk – known also as the garefowl – was a successful and thriving species. A huge, flightless bird – known to sailors as the 'penguin' – it laid but one egg a year, yet was abundant and perfectly adapted to its island and ocean life, living in large colonies and swimming great distances in search of food. It was a highly developed creature, turning fish into fat with great efficiency; it had few enemies and did no man and no beast any harm.

Islanders for centuries had 'farmed' the colonies of great auks, harvesting reasonable numbers of eggs, grown birds and succulent young, for food; not seriously affecting the balance between life and death which is the first law of nature. Then commercial enterprise took a hand. In the space of less than three centuries, at a rate which reached its climax at the beginning of the nineteenth century, every great auk in the world was sought out and destroyed for commercial gain. By 1844, extermination was complete.

The tragic story of the garefowl has been fully chronicled elsewhere by expert ornithologists and historians. It should never be forgotten, though, for there are other species which have reached a state of perilously low population. Thank heaven there are now men who realize this and protect and encourage the rare ones with all their energies. It is as well that we should know, however, that the responsibility lies with each and every one of us. If we exterminate ourselves, that is our business, but we have no right to take the rest of the animal world with us or to destroy it or any part of it for our own selfish ends.

There remain, therefore, six Atlantic auks, all of which can fly. Their flight, for they have small wings in proportion to their bodies, is inefficient and only sustained to escape danger – a high frequency, whirring flight which seldom looks particularly certain or safe.

Most of the family breed in colonies on stack-tops or cliff ledges, though some breed in rock crevices or even holes. With one exception, they lay a single large, very pointed egg.

Auks are entirely confined to the northern hemisphere, their range extending from well inside the Arctic Circle to the lower temperate latitudes.

BIRDS OF THE ATLANTIC OCEAN

DOVEKIE

(Syn.: little auk)

Plautus alle

Wing span 12 inches.

This tiny bird with its small bill, dumpy body and minute, whirring wings, is very abundant in far northern latitudes.

The only other ocean bird it vaguely resembles is the diving petrel of the Antarctic, which, incidentally, is no relation whatever. The head, neck and upper parts are black. The underside is usually white, but, when in full breeding plumage, there is a black patch on the bird's breast. The bill is very small, thick and black. The legs, which are placed very far back so that the feet stick out beyond the tail in flight, are flesh-coloured. Immature birds resemble non-breeding adults, but are brown above rather than black.

Dovekies breed on most Arctic coasts, laying one bluish-white egg in a rock-hole or crevice. Colonies are sometimes large and crowded. In winter they disperse to sea and are by far the most pelagic of the auk family. Anywhere, from the ice-edge to a line joining New England and north Britain, they may be met with far out in the ocean, either singly or in large parties. They have been recorded as far south as Cuba and as far east, in the Mediterranean, as Italy. They are small and weak of flight and are subject to what the scientists call 'wrecks'. Severe storms blow considerable numbers well inshore and they are frequently reported from places far removed from the coast. Apart from these 'wrecks', which are usually associated with weather phenomena, little auks appear to indulge in what are known as 'flights'. These are abnormal but apparently intentional departures from the normal winter range and take large numbers of the birds inland on either side of the Atlantic for no apparent reason. Both 'wrecks' and 'flights' are a regular feature of the life of this super-abundant species.

RAZORBILL

(Syn.: razor-billed auk)

Alca torda

Wing span 27 inches.

Though much smaller, of course, and perfectly capable of flight, this is the member of the family which most resembles paterfamilias, the great auk. The head and back are black, with a narrow white line running from the bill to the eye. The underside is white and the legs, placed well aft, are black. The bill, the main recognition feature of the bird, is large, laterally flattened and vertically striped, black and white. The young have a smaller, unstriped bill.

When the tell-tale bill cannot be seen, two features distinguish it from the guillemot. The colour of the back is black not chocolate and, when the bird is swimming, which is more often than not, the tail is held cocked rather high. There is a thin white line across the wing.

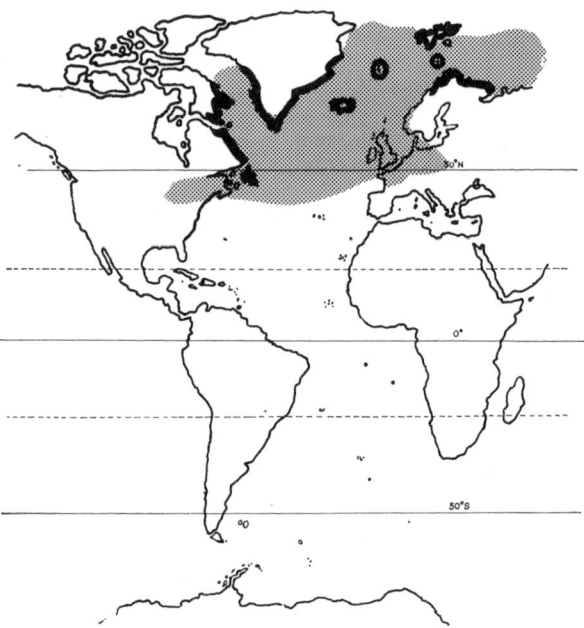
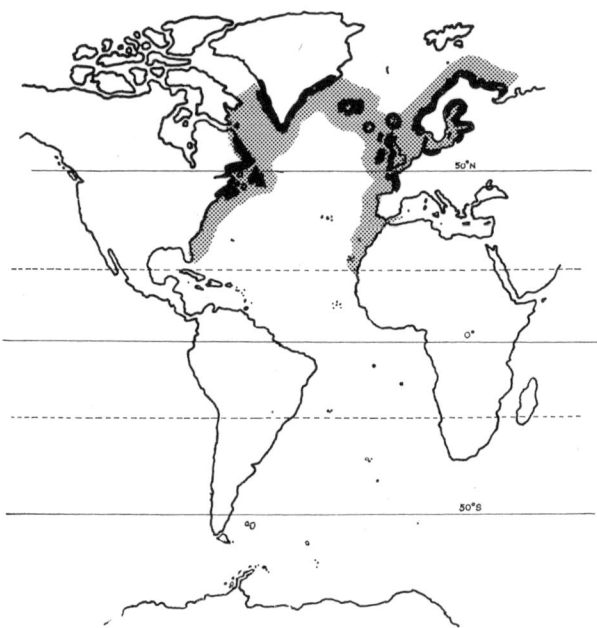

Razorbills nest in colonies, often with other sea birds, on cliffs or among rocks. They lay one blue-white or greenish-white egg in March or April. There are colonies from Greenland, south to Maine; on Iceland and the Faroes; in Britain and in Scandinavia; on the Brittany coast. In winter, razorbills spread throughout the Arctic seas and south as far as the Canaries or Florida.

GUILLEMOT

(Syns: common guillemot, common murre, Atlantic murre)

Uria aalge

Wing span 28 inches.

The synonym, murre, which is preferred by many eminent ornithologists, is an onomatopœic description of the growling, purring noise the bird makes. It has a very sharp, pointed bill, is chocolate brown above and white beneath, but otherwise resembles the razorbill. Some birds are strangely marked with a white ring around the eye, with a tangent white line running part of the way down the neck. These are known as bridled guillemots and are in no way racially or specifically separated from birds of orthodox colouring.

The guillemot breeds in huge colonies on cliff ledges or on flat stack-tops. The colonies are densely crowded, the birds standing upright, penguin-like and pressed closely together. Colonies may be found all around the north Atlantic wherever there are suitable cliffs and rocky islets, from Greenland to Spitzbergen and northern Scandinavia in the north, to Portugal and Maine in the south. A single, pale green or blue egg, well marked with brown and black, is laid any time from March until August, depending on the latitude.

Guillemots are seldom seen far from land. Of all the *Alcidae* they seem to suffer most from the terrible ravages of jettisoned fuel oil. Literally thousands of them are washed ashore every year, clogged and matted with oil – sometimes pathetic, still-living mummies with a struggling head peering out from a filthy black ball of coagulated muck – to die or be mercifully despatched by some humane human. Civilization! What a mockery of language is that word.

ARCTIC GUILLEMOT

(Syns: Brunnich's guillemot, thick-billed murre)

Uria lomvia

Wing span 31 inches.

The main difference in appearance between this species and the common guillemot is that it has a shorter, thicker bill, which has a pale line along the upper mandible, above the gape. The head, beak and upper parts are greyish-black, not chocolate. It is a slightly larger bird.

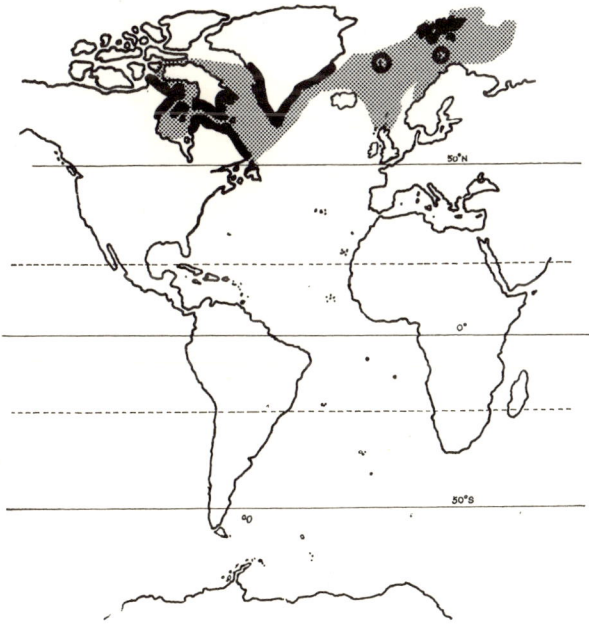

BIRDS OF THE ATLANTIC OCEAN

The Arctic guillemot, as the name implies, is a bird of the far north. On the eastern side of the Atlantic, it seldom comes south of Norway and, on the western side, seldom south of Maine. It is occasionally seen off the British Isles and as far south as northern Florida. It is a rather more pelagic species than either the common guillemot or the razorbill.

It breeds in dense colonies on cliffs, often in company with other auks. The eggs – each pair lays a single egg – are laid so close together that the birds are literally touching each other while incubating. Colonies are all in high latitudes, from the Gulf of St Lawrence north-eastward – Labrador, Greenland, Jan Mayen, Spitzbergen, Novaya Zemlya – keeping always in the regions of cold surface water and ice. Added to the guillemot vocabulary of purrs and growls is a sheep-like bleat.

BLACK GUILLEMOT

(Syns: tystie, sea pigeon)

Cepphus grylle

Wing span 22 inches.

Among Atlantic auks, this is the odd man out. Its proportions are less clumsy than the others, it flies with far greater ease and grace, it is the only one which lays more than one egg, and it is not particularly gregarious.

In breeding plumage, it is a very handsome bird. It is entirely black, except for a conspicuous white patch on each wing and bright red legs. The bill is slender and pointed. In winter, it is greyish-white with darker grey above. The white patch remains but is less conspicuous on the paler background. The young are similar to winter adults, but are speckled all over.

Tysties breed all around the Arctic Ocean, from New England to northern Greenland and Iceland, and from north-west Ireland and northern Scotland to Novaya Zemlya and Spitzbergen. They are not gregarious in their nesting habits, though many pairs breed in suitable sites. The two white, boldly blotched eggs are laid in a well-protected place, under a rock, in a rock crevice, among boulders or on a fairly inaccessible cliff ledge, usually near the water. Laying takes place in May or June.

Where black guillemots abound – for instance around the coastal islands of Maine – they can be seen swimming and diving, each pair sticking strictly to its own special area of water. They swim underwater well, feeding largely on shellfish, crabs and sand eels culled from the inshore, submerged rocks. Their voice is high-pitched and wheezy.

In winter, they spread southward, sometimes to northern France. They are, however, more abundant on the American side of the ocean where they reach as far south as the vicinity of New York.

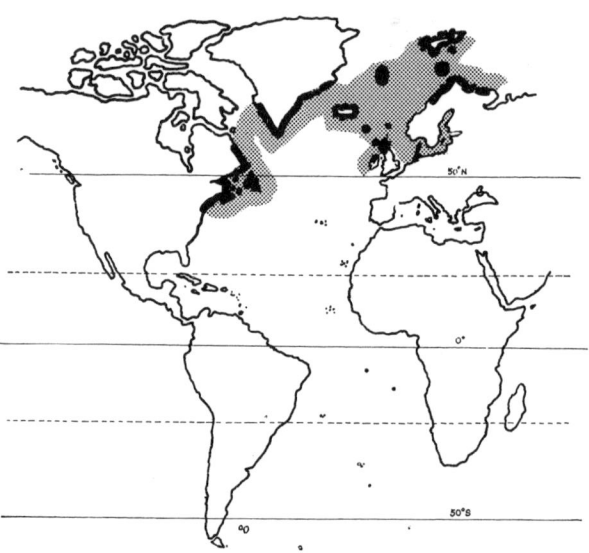

PUFFIN

(Syns: Atlantic puffin, sea parrot)

Fratercula arctica

Wing span 18 inches.

A more colourful little chap, you can hardly imagine. The puffin is certainly the gayest and funniest of the Atlantic auks. It is still a very common bird in northern latitudes, though there must be some anxiety about its continued abundance as a species because of the predations of man and his associates. The puffin is tame and can easily be approached. It lives in a hole, so is very susceptible to the ravages of rats and, to put it as mildly as possible, interference by cats and dogs. Many islands which used to abound with puffins now support but a few. And man is the villain of the piece – man or his camp followers.

A tubby, squat little bird with a black cap and a black collar, white undersides and a browny-grey back and mantle, the puffin's glory, in breeding garb, is its huge, triangular, multi-coloured bill and its bright orange feet. The bill diminishes and loses some of its brilliance in winter and immature birds have a small, nondescript one. The greyish-white cheeks are, however, always distinctive summer or winter, old or young.

Puffins breed, usually in colonies, in holes which are either old rabbit holes, disused petrel's burrows or self-burrowed holes, situated on earth-covered slopes overlooking the sea. They lay one white egg in a cavity which is lined with straw and feathers, a few feet from the entrance of the hole. The entrance is often concealed under a rock or boulder.

The breeding range stretches right round the northern Atlantic and Arctic Oceans, from Maine to Portugal. When not breeding puffins leave the vicinity of their breeding grounds and push well off out to sea. In winter, they may be seen as far afield as the Azores, the Canaries, the western Mediterranean, Bermuda and New York.

So heavy is the puffin when it is stuffed with fish that it has the greatest difficulty in taking off at all in calm conditions. If disturbed, it will thrash the water with its feet and fast-whirring wings in a desperate attempt to become airborne, which may take it a hundred yards or more before it finally gives up the struggle and plunges beneath the water with a final panic-stricken plop.

Unlike other auks, the puffin is strong on its legs; stands up well and runs strongly on land, with the body held nearly horizontal. What better known subject is there for the amateur colour photographer than a number of these beautiful little birds standing around near their nest burrows, some with several fish draped neatly, crosswise in their bills?

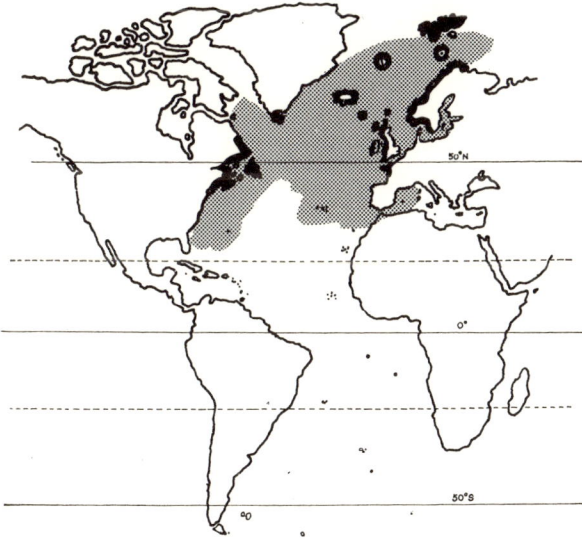

INDEX

Adélie Penguin 19, 21*
African Skimmer 135*, 144
Albatross, Black-browed 26, 29*
   Dark-mantled Sooty 28
   Grey-headed 28, 29*
   Light-mantled Sooty 30
   Royal 26, 29*
   Shy 27, 29*
   Sooty 28, 29*
   Wandering 24, 25*, 29*
   Yellow-nosed 28, 29*
Albatrosses 24
Alca torda 146
Alcidae, family 145
American Cormorant 79
American White Pelican 69, 71*
Anoüs (Gygis) albus 141
Anoüs minutus 141
Anoüs stolidus 140
Anoüs tenuirostris 141
Antarctic Fulmar 33*, 34
Antarctic Petrel 33*, 36
Antarctic Tern 133*, 134
Antarctic Whale-bird 40
Aptenodytes forsteri 17
Aptenodytes patagonica 19
Arctic Guillemot 143*, 147
Arctic Skua 16*, 96, 97*
Arctic Tern 132, 133*
Ascension Frigate Bird 85, 89*
Atlantic Murre 147
Atlantic Petrel 43
Atlantic Puffin 148
Audouin's Gull 105*, 107
Audubon's Shearwater 54
Auk, Great 17, 145
   Little 146
   Razor-billed 146
Auks 145

Bank Cormorant 80, 83*
Bearded Penguin 18, 21*
Bermuda Petrel 46
Bigua Cormorant 79
Black-bellied Storm Petrel 60, 61*
Black-browed Albatross 26, 29*
Black-capped Petrel 46
Black Guillemot 143*, 148
Black-headed Gull 112, 113*, 115*
Black Skimmer 139*, 144
Black-tailed Petrel 51
Black Tern 126, 129*
Blue-eyed Cormorant 82
Blue-eyed Shag 82, 83*
Blue-faced Booby 75, 77*
Blue Petrel 33*, 38
Boatswain-bird 66, 68
Bonaparte's Gull 113*, 116
Bonxie 98
Boobies 74
Booby, Blue-faced 75, 77*
   Brown 76, 77*
   Red-footed 75, 77*

Bridled Tern 128, 129*
British Storm Petrel 56, 61*
Broad-billed Prion 41*, 42
Broad-billed Whale-bird 42
Brown Booby 76, 77*
Brown Noddy 140
Brown Pelican 70, 71*
Brown-winged Tern 128
Brunnich's Guillemot 147
Bulweria bulwerii 47
Bulwer's Petrel 47, 49*

Cahow 45*, 46
Cape Cormorant 80, 83*
Cape Dove 51
Cape Gannet 75, 77*
Cape Hen 48
Cape Pigeon 32
Capped Petrel 46, 49*
Caspian Tern 135*, 138
Catharacta skua 98
Cayenne Tern 137
Cepphus grylle 148
Chinstrap Penguin 18
Chionididae, family 94
Chionis alba 94
Cinerous Shearwater 50
Cinnamon Skua 98
Common Cormorant 79, 83*
Common Diving Petrel 63, 67*
Common Guillemot 147
Common Gull 105*, 106, 109*
Common Murre 147
Common Noddy 135*, 140
Common Shearwater 54
Common Tern 133*, 136
Cormorant, American 79
   Bank 80, 83*
   Bigua 79
   Blue-eyed 82
   Cape 80, 83*
   Common 79, 83*
   Double-crested 78, 83*
   European 79
   Green 81
   Magellan 81
   Mexican 79
   Olivaceous 79, 83*
   Red-legged 82
   Reed 83*, 84
Cormorants 78
Cory's Shearwater 49*, 50
Crested Tern 138

Damara Tern 129*, 130
Dark-mantled Sooty Albatross 28
Diablotin 46
Diomedea cauta 27
Diomedea chlororhynchos 28
Diomedea chrysostoma 28

Diomedea epomophora 26
Diomedea exulans 24
Diomedea fusca 28
Diomedea melanophris 26
Diomedea palpebrata 30
Diomedeidae, family 24
Diver, Falkland 63
Diving Petrel, Common 63, 67*
   Fuegian 64
   Magellan 64, 67*
   South Georgia 64
Diving Petrels 63
Dolphin Gull 108, 113*, 115*
Dominican Gull 100, 105*, 109*
Double-crested Cormorant 78, 83*
Dovekie 143*, 146
Dove Prion 40, 41*
Dusky Shearwater 52

Elegant Tern 137
Emperor Penguin 17, 21*
Eudyptes chrysolophus 18
Eudyptes crestatus 20
European Cormorant 79

Fairy Prion 33*, 39
Falkland Diver 63
Fire Bird 60
Forster's Tern 130, 133*
Franklin's Gull 117*, 122
Fratercula arctica 148
Fregata aquila 85
Fregata ariel 88
Fregata magnificens 86
Fregata minor 86
Fregatidae, family 85
Fregetta tropica 60
Frigate Bird, Ascension 85, 89*
   Great 86, 89*
   Lesser 88, 89*
   Magnificent 86, 87*, 89*
Frigate Birds 85
Frigate Petrel 59
Fuegian Diving Petrel 64
Fulmar 34, 35*
Fulmar, Antarctic 33*, 34
   Giant 31, 33*
Fulmarinae, sub-family 31
Fulmars 31
Fulmarus (Daption) capensis 32
Fulmarus glacialis 34
Fulmarus glacialoides 34
Fulmarus (Thalassoica) antarcticus 36

Gannet 73*, 74
Gannet, Cape 75, 77*
   Northern 74

*Illustration

Gannets 74
Garrodia nereis 60
Gentoo Penguin 20, 21*
Giant Fulmar 31, 33*
Glaucous Gull 102, 105*, 109*
Great Black-backed Gull 102
Great Black-headed Gull 110, 117*
Greater Shearwater 51
Great Frigate Bird 86, 89*
Great Skua 97*, 98
Great-winged Petrel 41*, 42
Green Cormorant 81
Grey-backed Storm Petrel 60, 61*
Grey-headed Albatross 28, 29*
Grey-headed Gull 118, 121*
Grey Petrel 51
Grey Phalarope 90, 93*
Guillemot, Arctic 143*, 147
    Black 143*, 148
    Brunnich's 147
    Common 147
Guillemots 143*, 147
Gull, Audouin's 105*, 107
    Black-headed 112, 113*, 115*
    Bonaparte's 113*, 116
    Common 105*, 106, 109*
    Dolphin 108, 113*, 115*
    Dominican 100, 105*, 109*
    Franklin's 117*, 122
    Glaucous 102, 105*, 109*
    Great Black-backed 102, 105*, 109*
    Great Black-headed 110, 117*
    Grey-headed 118, 121*
    Hartlaub's 118
    Herring 101*, 104, 109*
    Iceland 103, 105*, 109*
    Ivory 110, 113*, 115*
    Kelp 100
    Kumlien's 103
    Laughing 121*, 122
    Lesser Black-backed 105*, 106, 109*
    Little 111, 113*, 115*
    Magellan 108
    Mediterranean 117*, 123
    Mew 106
    Ring-billed 105*, 107, 109*
    Ross's 111, 113*, 115*
    Sabine's 110, 113*, 115*
    Silver 118, 121*
    Slender-billed 116, 121*
    Southern Black-backed 100
    Thayer's 103, 105*
Gull-billed Tern 135*, 140
Gulls 100

Hagdon 51
Haglet 52
Halobaena caerulea 38
Hartlaub's Gull 118
Herald Petrel 41*, 44
Herring Gull 101*, 104, 109*
Hydrobates pelagicus 56
Hydrobatidae, family 56

Iceland Gull 103, 105*
IMPENNES, order 17
Ivory Gull 110, 113*, 115*

Jackass Penguin 21*, 22
Jaeger, Long-tailed 98
    Parasitic 96
    Pomarine 95

Kelp Gull 100
Kerguelen Petrel 41*, 44
King Penguin 19, 21*
King Shag 82
Kittiwake 119*, 120
Kumlien's Gull 103

Large-billed Tern 124, 129*
Laridae, family 100
Larinae, sub-family 100
LARO-LIMICOLAE, order 90
Larus argentatus 104
Larus (Atricilla) atricilla 122
Larus (Atricilla) melanocephalus 123
Larus (Atricilla) pipixcan 122
Larus audouinii 107
Larus canus 106
Larus (Chroicocephalus) cirrhocephalus 118
Larus (Chroicocephalus) geneï 116
Larus (Chroicocephalus) novaehollandiae 118
Larus (Chroicocephalus) philadelphia 116
Larus (Chroicocephalus) ridibundus 112
Larus delewarensis 107
Larus dominicanus 100
Larus fuscus 106
Larus glaucoides 103

Larus (Hydrocoloeus) minutus 111
Larus hyperboreus 102
Larus (Ichtyaëtus) ichtyaëtus 110
Larus marinus 102
Larus (Pagophila) eburneus 110
Larus (Rhodostethia) roseus 111
Larus (Rissa) tridactylus 120
Larus scoresbii 108
Larus thayeri 103
Larus (Xema) sabini 110
Laughing Gull 121*, 122
Leach's Fork-tailed Petrel 58
Leach's Petrel 58
Leach's Storm Petrel 57*, 58
Least Tern 126
Lesser Black-backed Gull 106, 109*
Lesser Crested Tern 135*, 138
Lesser Frigate Bird 88, 89*

Lesser Noddy 141
Light-mantled Sooty Albatross 30
Little Auk 146
Little Gull 111, 113*, 115*
Little Shearwater 49*, 54
Little Tern 125*, 126
Long-tail 68
Long-tailed Jaeger 98
Long-tailed Skua 97*, 98
Love Tern 141

Macaroni Penguin 18, 21*
Macronectes giganteus 31
Madeiran Storm Petrel 58, 61*
Magellan Cormorant 81
Magellan Diving Petrel 64, 67*
Magellan Gull 108
Magellan Penguin 21*, 22
Magnificent Frigate Bird 86, 87*, 89*
Malagash 75
Man-o'-war Bird 86
Manx Shearwater 29*, 49*, 54
Marlin Spike 66
Mediterranean Gull 117*, 123
Mediterranean Shearwater 50
Mew Gull 106
Mexican Cormorant 79
Morus bassanus 74
Morus capensis 75
Murre, Atlantic 147
    Common 147
    Thick-billed 147

Night Bird 60
Night-hawk 51
Noddies 124
Noddy, Brown 140
    Common 135*, 140
    Lesser 140
    White-capped 135*, 140
Noddy Tern 140
North Atlantic Shearwater 50
Northern Gannet 74
Northern Phalarope 91

Oceanites oceanicus 59
Oceanodroma castro 58
Oceanodroma leucorhoa 58
Olivaceous Cormorant 79, 83*

Pachyptila belcheri 39
Pachyptila desolata 40

*Illustration

Pachyptila turtur 39
Pachyptila vittata 42
Pachyptilinae, sub-family 38
Pagodroma nivea 38
Parasitic Jaeger 96
Pediunker 49*, 51
Pelagodroma marina 59
Pelecanidae, family 69
Pelecanoides georgicus 64
Pelecanoides magellani 64
Pelecanoides urinatrix 63
Pelecanoididae, family 63
Pelecanus erythrorhynchos 69
Pelecanus occidentalis 70
Pelecanus rufescens 69
Pelican, American White 69, 71*
   Brown 70, 71*
   Pink-backed 69, 71*
Pelicans 69
Penguin, Adélie 19, 21*
   Bearded 18, 21*
   Chinstrap 18
   Emperor 17, 21*
   Gentoo 20, 21*
   Jackass 21*, 22
   King 19, 21*
   Macaroni 18, 21*
   Magellan 21*, 22
   Ringed 18
   Rockhopper 20, 21*
Penguins 17
Petrel, Antarctic 33*, 36
   Atlantic 43
   Bermuda 46
   Black-capped 46
   Black-tailed 51
   Blue 33*, 38
   Bulwer's 47, 49*
   Capped 46, 49*
   Frigate 59
   Great-winged 41*, 42
   Grey 51
   Herald 41*, 44
   Kerguelen, 41*, 44
   Leach's 58
   Leach's Fork-tailed 58
   Schlegel's 41*, 43
   Snow 37*, 38
   Soft-plumaged 41*, 43
   South Trinidad 44
   West Indian 46
   White-chinned 48
   White-faced 59
Petrels 48
Petrel Sambullidor 64
Phaëthon aethereus 66
Phaëthon lepturus 68
Phaëthontidae, family 66
Phalacrocoracidae, family 78
Phalacrocorax africanus 84
Phalacrocorax aristotelis 81
Phalacrocorax atriceps 82
Phalacrocorax auritus 78
Phalacrocorax capensis 80
Phalacrocorax carbo 79

Phalacrocorax gaimardi 82
Phalacrocorax magellanicus 81
Phalacrocorax neglectus 80
Phalacrocorax olivaceus 79
Phalarope, Grey 90, 93*
   Northern 91
   Red 90
   Red-necked 91, 93*
   Wilson's 91, 93*
Phalaropes 90
Phalaropodidae, family 90
Phalaropus fulicarius 90
Phalaropus lobatus 91
Phalaropus tricolor 91
Pimblico 54
Pink-backed Pelican 69, 71*
Pintado 32, 33*
Plautus alle 146
Pomarine Jaeger 95
Pomarine Skua 95, 97*
Pomatorhine Skua 95
Prion, Broad-billed 41*, 42
   Dove 40, 41*
   Fairy 33*, 39
   Thin-billed 33*, 39
Prions 38
Procellaria aequinoctialis 48
Procellaria cinerea 51
Procellaria diomedea 50
Procellariidae, family 31
Procellariinae, sub-family 48
Pterodroma arminjoniana 44
Pterodroma brevirostris 44
Pterodroma cahow 46
Pterodroma hasitata 46
Pterodroma incerta 43
Pterodroma macroptera 42
Pterodroma mollis 43
Puffin 143*, 148
Puffin, Atlantic 148
Puffinus assimilis 54
Puffinus gravis 51
Puffinus griseus 52
Puffinus puffinus 54
Pygoscelis adeliae 19
Pygoscelis antarctica 18
Pygoscelis papua 20

Razorbill 143*, 146
Razor-billed Auk 146
Red-billed Tropic bird 66, 67*
Red-footed Booby 75, 77*
Red-footed Shag 82
Red-legged Cormorant 82
Red-necked Phalarope 91, 93*
Red Phalarope 90
Reed Cormorant 83*, 84
Ring-billed Gull 105*, 107, 109*
Ringed Penguin 18
Rockhopper Penguin 20, 21*
Rock Shag 81, 83*
Roseate Tern 131*, 137
Ross's Gull 111, 113*, 115*
Royal Albatross 26, 29*

Royal Tern 135*, 138
Rynchopidae, family 142
Rynchops flavirostris 144
Rynchops nigra 144

Sabine's Gull 110, 113*, 115*
Sandwich Tern 133*, 137
Schlegel's Petrel 41*, 43
Sea Parrot 148
Sea Pigeon 148
Shag 81, 83*
Shag, Blue-eyed 82, 83*
   King 82
   Red-footed 82
   Rock 81, 83*
Shearwater, Audubon's 54
   Cinerous 50
   Common 54
   Cory's 49*, 50
   Dusky 52
   Greater 51
   Little 49*, 54
   Madeiran Little 56
   Manx 29*, 49*, 54
   Mediterranean 50
   North Atlantic 50
   Sooty 49*, 52
   Tristan Great 51, 53*
Shearwaters 48
Sheathbill 93*, 94
Shoemaker 48, 49*
Shy Albatross 27, 29*
Silver Gull 118, 121*
Skimmer, African 135*, 144
   Black 139*, 144
Skimmers 142
Skua 98
Skua, Arctic 16*, 96, 97*
   Cinnamon 98
   Dark 98
   Great 97*, 98
   Long-tailed 97*, 98
   Pomarine 95, 97*
   Pomatorhine 95
   Richardson's 96
   Southern 98
Skuas 95
Slender-billed Gull 116, 121*
Slender-billed Whale-bird 39
Snow Petrel 37*, 38
Soft-plumaged Petrel 41*, 43
Solan Goose 14
Sooty Albatross 28, 29*
Sooty Shearwater 49*, 52
Sooty Tern 127, 129*
South American Tern 136
Southern Black-backed Gull 100
Southern Skua 98
South Georgia Diving Petrel 64
South Trinidad Petrel 44
Spheniscidae, family 17
Spheniscus demersus 22
Spheniscus magellanicus 22

*Illustration

STEGANOPODES, order 66
Stercorariidae, family 95
Stercorarius longicaudus 98
Stercorarius parasiticus 96
Stercorarius pomarinus 95
Sterna anaetheta 128
Sterna balaenarum 130
Sterna dougallii 137
Sterna forsteri 130
Sterna fuscata 127
Sterna (Gelochelidon) nilotica 140
Sterna hirundinacea 136
Sterna hirundo 136
Sterna hybrida 127
Sterna leucoptera 127
Sterna nigra 126
Sterna paradisaea 132
Sterna (Phaetusa) simplex 124
Sterna (Sternula) albifrons 126
Sterna (Thalasseus) bengalensis 138
Sterna (Thalasseus) caspia 138
Sterna (Thalasseus) maxima 138
Sterna (Thalasseus) sandvicensis 137
Sterna trudeaui 130
Sterna vittata 134
Sterninae, sub-family 124
Storm Petrel, Black-bellied 60, 61*
    British 56, 61*
    Grey-backed 60, 61*
    Leach's 57*, 58
    Madeiran 58, 61*
    White-faced 59, 61*
    Wilson's 59, 61*
Storm Petrels 56
Sula dactylatra 75
Sula leucogastra 76
Sula sula 75
Sulidae, family 74
Swallow-tailed Tern 134

Tern, Antarctic 133*, 134
    Arctic 132, 133*
    Black 126, 129*
    Bridled 128, 129*
    Brown-winged 128
    Caspian 135*, 138
    Cayenne 137
    Common 133*, 136
    Crested 138
    Damara 129*, 130
    Elegant 137
    Forster's 130, 133*
    Gull-billed 135*, 140
    Large-billed 124, 129*
    Least 126
    Lesser Crested 135*, 138
    Little 125*, 126
    Love 141
    Noddy 140
    Roseate 131*, 137
    Royal 135*, 138
    Sandwich 133*, 137
    Sooty 127, 129*
    South American 133*, 136
    Swallow-tailed 134
    Trudeau's 130, 133*
    Whiskered 127, 129*
    White 135*, 141
    White-winged Black 127, 129*
Terns 124
Thayer's Gull 103, 105*
Thick-billed Murre 147
Thin-billed Prion 33*, 39
Tristan Great Shearwater 51, 53*
Tropic Bird, Red-billed 66, 67*
    White-tailed 65*, 68
    Yellow-billed 68
Tropic Birds 66
Trudeau's Tern 130, 133*

TUBINARES, order 24
Tystie 148

Uria aalge 147
Uria lomvia 147

Wandering Albatross 24, 25*, 29*
West Indian Petrel 46
Whale-bird, Antarctic 40
    Broad-billed 42
    Slender-billed 39
Whiskered Tern 127, 129*
White-capped Noddy 135*, 141
White-chinned Petrel 48
White-faced Petrel 59
White-faced Storm Petrel 59, 61*
White-tailed Tropic Bird 65*, 68
White Tern 135*, 141
White-winged Black Tern 127, 129*
Wideawake 127
Wilson's Phalarope 91, 93*
Wilson's Storm Petrel 59, 61*

Yellow-billed Tropic Bird 68
Yellow-nosed Albatross 28, 29*

*Illustration